THE REALITY OF REDEMPTION

BONIFACE A. WILLEMS

THE REALITY
OF REDEMPTION

HERDER AND HERDER

1970

HERDER AND HERDER

232 Madison Avenue, New York, N. Y. 10016

BURNS & OATES LIMITED

25 Ashley Place, London S. W. 1

Original edition: "Verlossing in Kerk en Wereld",
J. J. Romen & Zonen, Roermond, 1967.

Library of Congress Catalog Card No: 78 - 105366
First published in West Germany © 1970 Herder KG
Printed in West Germany by Herder

CONTENTS

PREFACE

The present phenomenon of "secularization" presents grave problems both to the Christian in his ordinary life and to the theologian in his studies. Over an ever-widening region, it appears that the Church no longer presents itself to many as their natural homeland. And even what is called redemption in the language of the Church seems to have lost some of its relevance and reality. There is every reason therefore to re-open discussion of these problems. In our present approach, we shall be more concerned with not fighting shy of the questions which are really imperative today than with a comprehensive treatment which might possibly lose touch with immediate realities. A necessary result of this approach is that several aspects will be omitted from the discussion.

The following book is based on an article which first appeared in the Dutch *Tijdschrift voor Theologie* 5 (1965), pp. 28–48, and was then published in the United States under the title of "Redemption as a Human Reality" (Glen Rock, 1966). The line of thought runs as follows. The sense of the need of redemption seems to have lost much of its keenness through the general process of secularization. Hence the first chapter had to be devoted to modern man's attitude to life, in the hope of providing points of contact at which the preaching of redemption could be a live issue. Then, since the life of faith as it is today has grown out of a tradition many centuries old, the second chapter had to deal with some important stages of a history which concerns us all, in which the important figures are St. Irenaeus and St. Anselm. In the key-chapter, the third, the reality of the redemption is shown in its connections with the origins of the Christian Church. The question, "Why is the Church still needed?", had then to be dealt with in the final chapter, all the more so because the process of secularization has brought this question to the fore in a still more acute form.

Boniface A. Willems

I

THE MEANING OF REDEMPTION

1. The rediscovery of man

Theology is widely discredited today. One of the reasons is that too many of the problems discussed by theology had little palpable reference to real life. This remoteness showed and still shows itself in many ways. For instance, theologians often pose their problems within a framework for which certain categories were worked out in the past. But once the public has ceased to be familiar with these once normal categories, they are no longer viable as an introduction to the elucidation of a problem in real life. Hence the whole subsequent discussion hangs in the air, without concrete contacts with the facts and questions which men encounter in their own experience. A remarkably clear instance of this may be seen in a recent book on the redemption. The author begins his considerations by putting a question which he regards as central: does redemption imply a ransom?[1] But such a question can be felt as a real one only by those who have had a training in the technical questions of theology which

[1] Cf. J. Galot, La rédemption, mystère d'Alliance (1965).

cannot possibly be assumed for the vast majority of readers. It also supposes a certain acquaintance with the scriptural way of speaking about redemption, and with the reasons which led the Fathers and the theologians of the Middle Ages to put the question in these terms. When one has gained a certain amount of insight into all these matters, it is perhaps possible to recognize how central the question in fact may be. But this approach to theology reveals a feature of theology which is only being very slowly eliminated, and that is its "clericalism". A clergy which has been educated in a carefully-guarded isolation, sheltered by the folios of theological tradition, still possesses a quasi-monopoly of theological training. The number of laymen who can claim to be genuine theologians can be counted on the fingers of one hand. And where lay theologians do come forward, they are usually greeted with suspicion. One of the results of all this is the distance between much of theology and real life. The clergy lacked a sense of ordinary life, and had instead a sort of clerical experience of existence, so that what the clergy felt as a problem could at best be recognized as such by the laity when they had been slowly and painfully trained.

Then, for want of real experience, or by reason of the one-sidedness of clerical experience, many of the problems posed by theologians remained typically cerebral. These scholars were apparently more alert to certain contradictions which appeared among the historically current categories than to the difficulties of reconciling human experience and gospel message, which could at times be searching enough. All this brought with it a process which we may perhaps call — without falling into the trap of a neo-clericalism — the de-kerygmatizing of theology.

By this we mean that theology had ceased to be part of the living preaching of the Church directed to the life of man, and had become an introvert ecclesiastical preoccupation carried on behind the closed doors of a study. The theologians had lost sight of their public.

It sometimes happens that theologians also start not so much from historical categories as from some genuinely human question. But it should be remembered that the questions are not always the same. There are human questions which were prominent in earlier times but which have now either disappeared or are put in different terms. The easy supposition that all problems are of eternal value betrays a certain naivety, though it is true that some fundamental questions continue to recur. But whether the question is a fundamental one or not needs to be investigated precisely in each case. And this can only be properly done when one is aware of the spontaneous or considered questions which men today are asking themselves. To accept too light-heartedly that problems of earlier times still live on exposes theology to the danger of being lost in a fog and of really addressing nobody. The urgent demand made upon theology, that it should first make sure that it is dealing with real problems, presupposes much sensitivity to the outlook on life which is really that of the men among whom it lives. The past isolation of Church and theology was of no great benefit to the development of this outlook. It is precisely here that the breakthrough brought about by Vatican II as regards the notions of Church and world can be fruitful and stimulating. If it proves to be so, the alarms raised on so many sides may have to be reconsidered.

The investigation of the really live questions which are the starting-points of a really kerygmatic theology needs to be carried on with the greatest possible care and even reverence. Here too there is always the danger that a theologian, cost what it may, will pronounce a need to exist whose only real function is to prop up the weight of his system or perhaps give some purpose to his own life. There can often be subtle self-deception here, as Camus was clear-sighted enough to note, in one of the interviews undergone by his "Stranger": "He stood there and asked me whether I believed in God. I said I did not. He sat down, disconcerted. He said that it was impossible. Everyone believed in God, even if they had turned away from his face. This was his firm conviction, and if he ever had doubts about it, his whole life would be meaningless. 'Do you want my life to be meaningless?', he shouted at me. As I understood things, that was none of my business and I told him so. But he leaned across the table and shoved a crucifix under my nose, shouting at me as if he had lost his senses: 'I'm a Christian. I ask him to pardon your sins. You have to believe that he suffered for you.' I had not missed the point that he had used the friendly 'tu' when speaking to me, but I had had enough of it all. He grew more and more heated. As always happens when I want to get rid of someone whom I find it hard to listen to, I gave the impression of agreeing with him. He thought, to my surprise, that he had convinced me." [2] The need of God is here taken for granted because the speaker's way of life supposed it. If the stranger felt no such need, the theology of the interviewer and apparently even his whole life collapses at once. Here apologetics is inspired by fears and hence

[2] A. Camus, *L'Étranger*, E. T.: *The Stranger* (1946).

can even be charged with indignation. Such emotional self-justification has no idea of what is really going on in other people's minds.

When we consider in particular what Christian theology means by "redemption", it is well to realize the shifts of meaning that have taken place in recent years. Redemption supposes — if it is to be a really "human" and not a merely physical happening — that there is a desire for redemption. Men cannot be redeemed against their will. Animals may be, but not men. Christian apologetics sometimes presupposes all too hastily the desire for redemption. But modern man is once more preoccupied with discovering himself and the earth around him. As long as it is at all possible, he wishes to remain true to earth. God or gods who deprive him of part of his responsibility he distrusts. This undertaking was encouraged by the leading theologians, at least after a first reaction of horror. At any rate, the rediscovery of the sovereignty of man did not lead to the death of God but to the unmasking of an idol. A God who clutches convulsively at a patch of ground as his royal domain, who has to intervene at set intervals personally on earth to rearrange things according to his taste, is not the transcendent and omnipotent God of the Bible. His honour is not served by men's being deprived of part of their own responsibilities. If he needed such service, he would ultimately be degraded into a competitor with man and would seem to be on the same level as man. As long as miracles are "the dearest children of faith" man has failed to discover the miracle of his own being and hence the miracle of God himself. The number of the mourners who are verifying the prophecy of Nietzsche by still secretly visiting at midnight the grave of their dead God, is shrinking visibly. This God, pronounced dead, is now generally seen to have been only a *deus ex machina*, a projection of human needs, only invoked when all human help failed. This sort of faith, which was naive to say the most of it, was sometimes actually considered to be particularly pious. There is no need to condemn earlier generations from the loftier point of view of our own times. But it is legitimate to point out that this sort of piety can switch over very quickly into its less pious opposite. In any case, this *deus ex machina* can very quickly take over the function of an alibi whenever men fail to meet their responsibilities on earth. This has been put very clearly by Simone de Beauvoir, though she was not the first to think of it.[3] Edmund says in King Lear: "This is the excellent foppery of the world that when we are sick in fortune — often the surfeit of our own behaviour — we make guilty of our disasters the sun, the moon and the stars; as if we were villains by necessity, fools by heavenly compulsion, knaves, thieves, and treachers by spherical predominance, drunkards, liars and adulterers by an enforced obedience of planetary influence; and all that we are evil in, by a divine thrusting on ..."[4]

As the notion of the divine transcendence becomes more and more explicit, and God appears less and less as a sort of competitor with man, the starting-point for a doctrine of redemption becomes harder to find. Man sees himself as created according to the image of God. The earth belongs to man. When St Paul says that nature hopes to be freed one day from the slavery of corruption and to share the freedom and the

[3] S. de Beauvoir, *Pour une moralité de l'ambiguité* (6th ed., 1948).
[4] *King Lear*, Act I, scene 2.

glory of the children of God,[5] he sees the world as a prolongation of man in his bodily nature. If man lives in accordance with his task, this harmony is reflected in the world around him; if man fails, his disorder impinges on the world. This is clearly not a view of the world which is based on physics or biology. It sees the world as full of human characteristics. This view of the world and man as united in one destiny is very clearly expressed in the Book of Genesis. Before the Fall, we read the commandment of God: "Be fruitful and multiply, and fill the earth and subdue it; and have dominion over the fish of the sea and over the birds of the air and over every living thing that moves upon the earth."[6] Immediately after the Fall, however, we read: "Cursed is the ground because of you ... Thorns and thistles it shall bring forth for you... In the sweat of your face you shall eat bread."[7] The destiny of earth is entrusted to the free will of man. It was cursed along with man and it can be created anew along with man. "The lion shall eat straw like the ox, the suckling child shall play over the hole of the asp, and the weaned child shall put his hand on the adder's den" (Is 11 : 7 f.).

But if man is responsible for the earth as his proper domain, it would be a precarious undertaking to try to demarcate within this totality of human effort any need for God and his redemption which could be localized in a special part of the world. Those who are inclined to point to natural catastrophes, sickness and epidemics would do well to remember that even such phenomena are in principle subject to human control. It was God's will, Vatican II affirms, to leave man "in the hand of

[5] Cf. Rom 8 : 19 ff.   [6] Gen 1 : 28.   [7] Gen 3 : 17–19.

15

his own counsel".[8] Hence an earthquake or the threat of atomic war should not impel men in the first instance to rush to the church in crowds to ask God to avert such dangers. When the house is on fire we call the fire-brigade, not the local clergy. The threats which loom over mankind today should inspire Christians to effort on the professional and technical level at least as much as on the level of prayer. Our task of humanizing the world, which we acknowledge as set us by God, should be one of our strongest motives. Many of the objections raised against Christianity sprang from the fact that we fled too hastily to seek the help of God and his saints, and regarded this as a substitute for the tools which God had put in our own hands.

2. *The mystery of man*

In the search for a concrete, experimental starting-point for a soteriology, it has become fairly clear that no real need of redemption can be found on the "horizontal" dimension. Or at least, "horizontally", in the dimension of human life on earth, there are no regions of need where man is exclusively thrown back on God. There are no demonstrably restricted areas where God has on principle reserved matters to himself. It is remarkable, nevertheless, that throughout the whole of human history clear expressions have never been wanting to give impressive voice to man's desire for redemption. The great classical authors

[8] Hence the Pastoral Constitution of Vatican II on the Church in the Modern World, art. 17, quotes Ecclus 15:14 for man's authority, as image of God, over creation; cf. arts. 12 and 34 of the Constitution.

of the world's literature have come back again and again to what is evidently one of the primary urges of man. The Ajax of Sophocles tries to soothe the anger of Athene: "I go to the baths, to the pools by the bank of the river, and I shall wash away my stains and escape the fierce anger of the goddess" [9] — the ancient gesture which Lady Macbeth repeats. [10] And in Hemingway's *For Whom the Bell Tolls*, there is an old man, described with evident sympathy, who affirms that the civil war and all its blood-letting will have to be expiated by great penance — civil if not religious — because otherwise there can be no sound basis for human life. [11] When we consider the concrete efforts which man has made to attain redemption, and the concrete means which he has used in the effort, it seems that we have all the raw material for a process of de-mythologization.

But the question remains as to whether all these myths, decipherable no doubt in the concrete as projections, do not still point to a fundamental situation of human life, a radical element in the structure of man's existence. [12] The sense of human insufficiency, which is attested to in so many ways in literature, constantly points to fear, guilt and isolation. Basically, it is the same fear which was at the origin of Greek tragedy and which came to light in another form in the mystery

[9] Sophocles, *Ajax*, lines 654–6.
[10] *Macbeth*, Act V, scene 1.
[11] E. Hemingway, *For Whom the Bell Tolls*.
[12] Jaspers criticizes certain forms of demythologization as depriving us of all our world of myth and emptying the realm of symbol, and thus silencing the language of transcendence which is so rich in meanings. Cf. K. Jaspers, *Der philosophische Glaube angesichts der Offenbarung* (1962), E. T.: *Philosophical Faith and Revelation* (1967).

religions of the Greek and Roman world. The search is always for "sôteria" — salvation, rescue, redemption. The mysterious rites, for all their sometimes bizarre divergencies, may be ultimately seen as an almost despairing attempt to enter into fellowship with the godhead. The human lot had no doubt been projected into the life of the god, but so had the conquest of destiny, and it was this which the worshipper longed to share. This anxious question about salvation was first directed outwards. Nature and the divine were objects, to be dealt with as possible threats. If they could be reconciled, redemption was achieved. But with the coming of profounder insight into human freedom and human autonomy, the direction of the question changed and it was posed to the inwardness of man's own self. The menacing gods outside now began to appear as projections of something which lay within man himself, his freedom. Dostoievsky has given this fact a very vivid expression. In *The Possessed*, Kirilov is shown as taking the first but decisive step. "Is there really no one on this planet, now that we have dismissed God and believe in our free will, who will have the courage to show that he is fully free?" "I was three years looking for this attribute of my godhead and now I have found it. It is my free will." The impact of this discovery of human freedom now transfers the centre of the threatening typhoon into the heart of man. Dostoievsky notes this consequence. If man's freedom is of this nature, he has to be free even as regards existence or non-existence. The absurd conclusion of this self-discovery is suicide. It is the only way in which man can really be God. When Stepanovitch asks Kirilov, "If you shoot yourself you will be a god, won't you?", Kirilov answers, "Yes, then I shall be a god."

Thus we are faced once more with a central human question, but put in a radical way. Is there still room, in principle, for need of redemption in man as a free, autonomous being? Does human freedom itself, more than anything else perhaps, reveal a trait which we could call the desire for redemption? At the very moment when man is becoming more and more fully conscious of his freedom, he is also learning to recognize that human freedom itself displays an insuperable ambiguity. The mystery reflected by human freedom has often been indicated by Jaspers.[13] Consideration of our freedom points to absolute and self-sufficient freedom. Our freedom really tolerates no restrictions and hence tends — as will — to absolute power. But men are equally well aware that this absolute freedom and this absolute omnipotence are an illusion as far as man is concerned. Obviously, it is not thanks to his own will that man is what he is, a free person. In principle, man's freedom means that he can creatively direct his own life and hence his portion of the world. But the very origin of the whole process, the possibility of radical freedom which is man's own self, is not produced by man himself but is given him. Even a writer so anti-metaphysical and anti-mythological as Harvey Cox seems to take this for granted. Man can only be responsible, he affirms, if he responds to someone. One has to be responsible *for* something *to* somebody. To be free and responsible, that is, to be a man, man has to give an answer to some being that is not man.[14] This being which bestows us on ourselves and which comes to light in the analysis of human freedom is what

---

[13] K. Jaspers, *op. cit.*, passim; and cf. Vatican II, "Pastoral Constitution on the Church in the Modern World", art. 10.
[14] Harvey Cox, *The Secular City* (1965).

we call God. He is not the jealous rival of our human freedom but the source from whose gift our freedom perpetually springs. All the myths and all the imagery in which man proclaims that he is not alone in the universe (Unamuno) are concrete illustrations of this basic human situation. Man *has* no need of a transcendent God. He *is*, essentially, need of him.

This basic situation of man could be summed up rather flatly by calling it a mystery. To call man a mystery is, however, nothing very banal for those who are acquainted with the technical terms of theology. Here, as is well known, the word "mystery" originally had a very pregnant sense. A mystery is an enigma because in the mysterious visible reality something else which is not directly visible is now embodied. In this sense the human body is a "mystery" — the mystery in which the whole person visibly enters the world of experience. In the same way every special human gesture, such as facial expression, hand-shake or kiss, is the embodiment of a mood or sentiment in which the whole man is present for the moment.

Now the real threat which we constantly experience is that of infringing on the mystery of our own existence. We do this when we draw a tight circle round our own existence and make ourselves self-sufficient. We regard ourselves in the absolute and exclusive sense as the one standard of everything and everybody. The presence of the Other who is at the centre of human freedom and gives us to ourselves is ignored. The inclination to barricade ourselves behind this attitude is perhaps not too difficult to explain. The "Other" cannot be seen in his own, proper form. He is always concealed under the mysterious veil of a finite, human freedom. The transcendent God is "wholly other" and cannot be encountered apart, like one earthly object among others.

But we do meet other men and we have all sorts of relationships with them, personal and material. The discussion of personal relationships has been very much to the fore since the coming of existentialism. We owe it the dogma of "existence-with-others". This is a gain. When we recognize another man as "other", we admit that his way of existing within my life is not dependent on *my* freedom. As soon as we begin to take the "otherness" of a man seriously, we already proclaim that we are not the absolute measure of all things. But like all dogma, deeper questions may be posed here. Why should I really not try to incorporate the other, like any other random object, into the companionable but closed house of my own free existence? Why should I not make a slave of him if he lends himself to the process? Ultimately, no other reason can be given why I should not try to "manipulate" another man except the recognition that he too is the manifestation and embodiment of Someone who is above us all. By acknowledging the mystery of the other we admit implicitly that we believe in the mystery of the "Other-in-myself".

Under these circumstances we may describe "redemption" as: allowing the other to approach us. Note that we now write "other" without a capital letter. Within this world we are dealing with other men whom we respect and allow into our existence. But we also believe that this is only possible when we believe (implicitly or explicitly) that the other is a mystery — a manifestation of the transcendent Other who is God. Thus redemption is the acceptance and reverence of the otherness of our fellows. And it is this reverence which creates fellowship, or, in ecclesiastical terms, salvation. By respecting others one overcomes the basic form of all sinfulness, which is none other than egoism. The closed circle round one's own self as the sole and central focus of existence is broken and an ellipse ensues with two focuses. In the present state of human society this is a matter which demands close attention. The happy discovery of human autonomy on the horizontal or earthly level can lead to and does in fact lead to the emergence of a new type of *homo faber*. This is creative man who freely takes his destiny into his own hands and with his computers and space-ships turns the earth into a great stepping-stone for man. It is a great blessing that Christians too are now becoming fully conscious of this task which was too often neglected. But it would be disastrous if our creativity were to be developed at the expense of the conviction that it can only be a truly human activity when the mystery of the other is recognized. Even Cox, in spite of all his enthusiasm for the "coming of age" of the world which he described, has to insist that this only makes artists and poets more necessary than ever. When the mystery of the other is not respected, *homo faber* succumbs to a "Dionysiac" intoxication which is full of danger. It is destructive because violation or elimination of the otherness of men involves in fact the de-humanization of the world. It was apropos of this danger that Jaspers warned against "revolution as a principle of life".[15] When inhumanity threatens to become general, happily there are always forces which react spontaneously at once. Impersonalism is countered by the revolt of *homo ludens* who insists on his right to his "happenings" at all costs.

---

[15] K. Jaspers, *Philosophical Faith and Revelation*, ad fin.

Only the believer, who may be said to include here, however, the man with a merely "philosophical faith", is really able to make room for the other qua other. But this can hardly be done without a conversion, a renewal of the heart such as the Bible understands under the term *metanoia*. It is the act in which man loses himself in order to rediscover himself, renounces himself and surrenders himself to the mystery of the other. At the beginning, this is of course felt only as loss. Part of our autonomy is taken away so that the other may enter our world. But this is a very general phenomenon which is not confined to certain dramatic moments. It needs no very wide experience to teach us that life is "giving and taking". If such experiences have been intense, we recognize that the same human reality is involved of which the Gospel speaks when it says that the grain of wheat which falls into the earth must die. This text fascinated Dostoievsky so much that he used it as the motto for his most profoundly human novel, *The Brothers Karamazov*. That he who dies (at least a little) can still rise again is a grace, a gift from elsewhere. One rediscovers oneself in the grace of others. This is the only real resurrection of freedom and creativity, by which it becomes its own authentic self, rid of all lust for power and urge of possessiveness, and just striving respectfully to create living space. This is what Steinbeck recognized when he said: "Perhaps you are not really yourself until you have really given yourself to someone else." [16]

It is the faith of Christians that the "wholly other" who is God has revealed himself in many ways in the past as in the present. His most concrete revelation is the man beside me.

[16] J. Steinbeck, *Sweet Thursday*.

Christians also believe that God has revealed himself in a unique way in the life and death of one man, Jesus Christ. Hence redemption, the breaking out from isolation, is our encounter with the Christ who accepted so consistently his being-for-others that he was brought thereby to his death. But his death was the death of the grain of wheat which multiplies a hundredfold. — Or is this only a pious traditional phrase? Is it perhaps even an attempted evasion? Do I use the Jesus of history to help me to forget the men who live beside me, perhaps in misery? It is often said, of course, that Jesus is our contemporary, but is this something that can be really made credible? And can it be made true in such a way that he never interferes with our actual attention to those who live beside us?

3. The problem of interpretation

The questions at the end of the last paragraph are not really as new as they may seem. But here too we must make our way through a thicket of tangled words, if we are to discover how the problem really existed in earlier times.

Theologians who discussed explicitly the doctrine of the redemption made a distinction (which is still in use) between "objective" and "subjective" redemption. The first term was meant to emphasize beyond all doubt that redemption had taken place once and for all. The second term dealt with the fact that men of the present day, living two thousand years after Christ, are redeemed. The paradox, which appears to unprejudiced observers to be intrinsic to the juxtaposition of the two statements, that redemption took place once and for all in Jesus and that redemption is accomplished here and now, was thought to be resolved by the introduction of this distinction into the notion of redemption.

A number of authors are content simply to repeat this distinction and give it a very general explanation. It is said, for instance, that the redemption of the human race is called "objective redemption", to which Jesus the redeemer had a strict right, and Mary a right in a more secondary way. The application of this deliverance and renovation to individual men is called "subjective redemption".[17] But there too we are left to ask what is the precise meaning of this nominal solution. Why, for instance, does this distinction, introduced with apparently so little misgivings, not lead to a sort of infinite series? Why do we never speak of an application of the application and so on *ad infinitum*?

Others give what is really the same answer when they maintain that the *act* of Christ in redeeming man is redemption in the objective sense, while the application of the consequences of this act to individuals, through which their redemption is realized, is redemption in the subjective sense.[18] We are given the impression that redemption is thought of as the process whereby Christ gathered, through his life and death, a sort of arsenal of redemptive power. Then a new process is called for so that these powers may in fact be brought into use in the course of history for the benefit of individual men. But this way of looking at things also provides difficulties. We see that a truly human event is interpreted almost as a mechanism. Human and personal categories are replaced by categories which seem

[17] e. g. R. Garrigou-Lagrange, *De Christo Salvatore* (1946), p. 412.
[18] J. Pohle, *Dogmatic Theology*, V (Soteriology).

rather to be taken from non-living matter. But present-day theology is really endeavouring to break through this "physicism" in which what is human in the strict sense is thought of and described with the help of categories from nature. Present-day tendencies go right in the opposite direction, justifiably, as we have seen in our previous discussion. Scripture too reverses the process, and speaks of nature in categories which are borrowed from the strictly human. But the concept of objective redemption as "the merits gained once and for all by the redeemer" and the subjective redemption as the "communication of these merits to the individual redeemed"[19] suggests too strongly that merit is a sort of substance which can be isolated by man, a sort of chemical product which can be stored away somewhere. If necessary or desirable this supply can be drawn on subsequently.

Some authors have tried to give a clear account of the distinction between objective and subjective redemption. Scheeben, who was one of the first to make use of this terminology, appealed expressly to Scripture in his explanation. He did not claim that Scripture spoke in so many words about "subjective" and "objective" redemption, but he based his argument on the fact that at times Scripture speaks of redemption as something already accomplished, while at other times it sees it as still to come.[20] But among present-day theologians one already encounters a certain diffidence. This is shown, for instance, in the fact that some affirm that redemption *in the strict sense* is exactly what has been described above as "subjective" redemption. They then go on to say that what is usually called

[19] A. d'Alès, *De Verbo Incarnato* (1930), p. 379.
[20] M. J. Scheeben, *Handbuch der katholischen Dogmatik*, V, pp. 1330–1.

"objective redemption" is the cause[21] or the principle[22] of redemption in the strict sense. A further step is to affirm that the objective redemption has no meaning except in so far as it is completed by the so-called subjective redemption.

When we try to clear away some of the obscurities which befog theology here, we find ourselves, it seems, concerned with some symptomatic shifts which are the result of a very deep-seated process of change. The concentration of attention on the "subjective redemption" is a typical example of how "modern" anthropology (actually introduced by Kant and Hegel) is gaining a hesitant footing in theology. As long as the "object" was naively considered to be an independent quantity juxtaposed to the subject, it was possible to be content in theology with a general and cautious "adaptation" of the traditional treatises. But when "nature", "history", and "objective fact" were only accepted as humanly meaningful in so far as they are also understood by man and absorbed into his thinking existence, immense demands were made on theological hermeneutics. Hermeneutics forces us to ask ourselves what "interpretation" of a word or an event from the past really means. In its simplest form, this question comes to the fore in the endless repetition of the Italian saying: *traduttore traditore* — the translator is always a traitor. How far does the special attitude of the interpreter, preacher or translator enter into the translation? Can a translator do anything else but interpret his own way of seeing things? It is impossible to discuss here the enormous complex of questions which arises at this point. We think, however, that the problems raised by the seemingly simple distinction between objective and

[21] F. M. Gallati, *Der Mensch als Erlöser und Erlöster* (1958), p. 40.
[22] J. Galot, *La rédemption, mystère d'Alliance* (1965), pp. 19 f.

27

subjective redemption are in fact a certain form of the general hermeneutical problem. The most radical solution of this problem is given when the whole of theology is considered to be only the translation into words of the "self-consciousness of the faithful". The doctrine of redemption then becomes only a facet of anthropology, just as the actual exercise of the act of faith is no more than a certain form of man's self-understanding, when he sees himself as directed towards the transcendent God. Then the reality of redemption consists exclusively of the acceptance in faith of the message of redemption.[23]

In so far as this radical reversal of thought makes us attentive to the fact that the events of redemption cannot be looked on as a sort of mechanism it is a salutary phenomenon. This is because the redemption is in fact an event with a specifically human meaning. But it now seems as though we had reached the point where the correct approach is being transformed into its opposite. The radical position which we have just described gives the impression that the unique events of Jesus' passion, death and resurrection are really only incidental and no longer deserve attention. All that matters is our present act of existence in so far as it is done in faith. Because and in so far as such a faith uses the narratives and symbols provided by the religious tradition of Christianity it can still be called the Christian faith. But then the question is: is any value still attributed to the historically unique and unrepeatable events of Christ's life and death, or is that just so much "ordinary history" and hence irrelevant, since the act of redemptive faith cannot be regu-

[23] F. Buri, *Christian Faith in our Time* (1966).

lated *per se* by any historical item? It is remarkable that at the present day this last extreme viewpoint is upheld chiefly by some Protestant theologians. This is remarkable because in ancient times the great protest of the Reformation against Rome was that Catholic theology was constantly seeking to diminish the unique and irreplaceable value of the mystery of Christ. Catholic ecclesiology, for instance, came under fire. Its doctrine of the Church as the mystical Body of Christ was seen as giving too much honour to the (present-day) Church, at the expense of the Lord whom the Church only had to *serve*. The general opinion also was that Catholic theology, in the matter of the sacraments and above all in the Last Supper and the Eucharist, did far less than justice to the uniqueness of the sacrifice of the cross. And more generally still, whenever the contrast of Scripture and tradition came up for discussion, many Reformed theologians thought that they had to defend energetically the principle of *Sola Scriptura,* against the unbridled self-will to which Rome offered a haven by giving so large a place to active tradition. In many ways Catholic theology showed that it was ready to take account of the authentic values expressed in these misgivings of Protestants. In particular, when discussing the relationship of Scripture and tradition, theologians were intent on bringing out the unique and irreplaceable position of Scripture — more clearly than often happens nowadays. But the radical principle which we have signalled has, as we have seen, a significance which may not be ignored.

From all this it appears that the whole situation has not become very much clearer in recent times. But with all due respect for the motives which have led to the extreme positions in modern Protestant theology, we must still take seriously the words of St Paul: "In Christ we have redemption through his blood, the forgiveness of our trespasses" (Eph 1 : 7). The life, death and resurrection of Christ constitute in fact what can be called the "objective" element of the redemption. But the term "objective" is not very happy. It seems to suggest a way of looking at the event of redemption which reduces the saving act of Christ to a "thing". Even when we note that the word "object" has the overtones of a relationship with a subject, it is still inadequate in the present situation. The mystery of the redemption in and through Christ is not an "object" of non-committed knowledge. The important point here is that the event of the redemption should, in one way or another constitute a summons to my own basic response. A man encounters numbers of "objects" every day of his life, to some of which he remains quite indifferent, while others claim more attention. Only in some cases does he feel himself fully engaged as a person, and when this is so, he is no longer said to be dealing with an "object". Such encounters are characterized by the need of an attitude different from that which occurs in the relationship of subject and object. The person whom a man encounters is not an "object". He is a unique and irreplaceable subject. Hence he cannot be arbitrarily made an "object" of my free acts and my free purposes without his own proper "otherness" being infringed upon. If redemption attains the profoundest levels of man, the redemption event must take place in the sphere of inter-personal encounter. It is not a process which has to be undergone, and it is not confined to any process of cognition, but it is the free gift of self from one person to another, whereby the other is given the choice of freely allowing his isolation to be ended. If he agrees to such an encounter he will be born again along with the other, after a "moment" of self-renunciation. Hence what the term "objective redemption" indicates is a free, personal act in which man is offered redemption and salvation through another.

Under these circumstances, it is obviously of supreme importance that the "other" who thus offers himself is really and truly another. As soon as we try to annex the other by loading him exclusively with our own purposes, he ceases to be another and is reduced to a mere reflection of our own selves. If the story of Jesus' saving deed becomes purely and exclusively an expression of my present-day notion of faith, the old thesis of Feuerbach has been revived in a new form, namely, that all religious concepts are in fact merely projections of human needs. But then one has at the same time undertaken a subtle effort at *self*-redemption. Nonetheless, even the most profound human "self-understanding" can only be arrived at in a real confrontation with a real "another". If one eliminates the reality of the other, one at once does away with all true self-understanding, since one is thrown back upon one's own isolated existence. If the other is not real, no encounter is possible, the isolation is not broken through and man is left to himself and to himself alone on the profoundest level.

Hence the words "objective" and "subjective" redemption characterize two poles which are necessary for a genuine encounter. One is the self-surrender of one person as the offering of salvation to another, and the other is the assent to this offer. We believe that this offering of redemption was embodied in a unique way in the life and death of Jesus of Nazareth. In him "the Other" comes to meet us. Throughout the course of Christian history, very different ways have been used to express

31

this central mystery, and the various descriptions given by Christian faith have naturally all been stamped by the societies and cultures from which they sprang. This is true of the New Testament writers and it is also true of later times. The question of how this unique offer of salvation still comes to us at the present day is not thereby answered. But after some considerations on the manner in which the redemptive offer of Christ was described, this question will demand once more an answer.

II

HISTORICAL SKETCHES

1. The message of the New Testament

The message of redemption through Jesus Christ was born of a historical event which took place once. In this message we are challenged with the truth that someone was "born of a woman" (Gal 4 : 4), died on a cross, and rose again for our sake. This is addressed to us as a challenge or summons — it is not merely reported as an item of news. The bearers of the message testified, sometimes in an exuberant fashion, to their belief. It is possible to consider that the historical content is not very important and still hold that this New Testament faith and its testimony presupposes the historicity of Jesus of Nazareth.[24] Then, for reasons which have been discussed in part above, it is sometimes supposed that this is the only fact which is presupposed in the testimony, which knows nothing of any more definite concrete details. Those who take this point of view are content with the fact that Jesus lived and died, but maintain that the actual course of his life cannot be traced and

[24] R. Bultmann, *Das Verhältnis der urchristlichen Christusbotschaft zum historischen Jesus* (1960), p. 9.

is in any case totally unimportant. But if redemption is something that comes from outside us, if it is accomplished by God in Jesus, and if man is not to think eventually in terms of a subtle form of self-redemption, we must not think of the content of the message, apart from the redemptive event, as wholly produced by faith itself.[25] The historical criticism of specialist exegesis can provide us with the proper methods for gaining a good idea of what is historical and what is certainly not historical. Furthermore, the exegetes find themselves compelled to leave a broad margin of uncertainty around their results. Such research does not make the "existential risk" of faith impossible, but it does prevent us taking humanly irresponsible steps which would only orientate us towards our "projections" or "idols". We believe that God was active in a very special way in the history of Jesus on this earth. Faith is thus given a historical and geographical orientation.

The whole of the New Testament is in fact inspired by one single theme, which recurs again and again in many variations: faith in redemption through Jesus Christ. The writings of the New Testament owe their origin precisely to this faith. The first group of disciples, who had been close witnesses of the extraordinary life of Jesus, were fully convinced that he must be the long expected Messiah. The scandalous end of Jesus' life raised doubts in their mind. The course of events has been preserved for us by the Lucan tradition. After the death of Jesus they were "sad" and disappointed, because the hopes they had cherished of Jesus being the redeemer of Israel seemed to have

---

[25] W. Pannenberg, *Jesus: God and Man* (1968); E. Lohse, "Die Frage nach dem historischen Jesus in der gegenwärtigen neutestamentlichen Forschung", *Theologische Literaturzeitung* 87 (1962), cols. 161–74.

faded (Lk 24 : 17–21). But their first sorely-tried hope became certainty when they became convinced that the Lord was really risen. In the oldest New Testament testimony to the resurrection St Paul puts forward the final argument when precision is called for: The Lord showed himself to more than five hundred brethren at once, "of whom most are still alive" (1 Cor 15 : 6). How precisely the apparition took place is not clear. Nonetheless, St Paul affirms in the sequel to this confession of faith that the encounter with the risen Lord is not to be considered a natural earthly event, just as resurrection and glorification cannot be regarded as a sort of natural process. "As there is a natural body, so too there is a spiritual body" (1 Cor 15 : 44), and the nature of the two realities is very different. Hence misunderstandings can arise when it is said that the risen Lord is our "contemporary". A new life began with the resurrection of Christ. His mortal existence on earth had come to an end.

Though the resurrection of the Lord was therefore not strictly an event within this world, St Paul and the whole first generation of Christians along with him did not hesitate for a moment to see in the resurrection the germ of our redemption. "If Christ is not risen from the dead, then our preaching is futile and your faith empty" — or, more precisely, "you are still in your sins" (1 Cor 15 : 14, 17). Some years later he writes very positively in the Letter to the Romans: "Jesus was raised up for our justification" (Rom 4 : 25). Filled with this certain faith, the first generation of Christians felt little need of studying the redemptive significance of the death of Jesus in itself. It was only gradually that believers felt themselves compelled to do this, in order to integrate the actual ending of Jesus' earthly life into the perspective of faith. As the notion penetrated their thought, they slowly arrived at the paradoxical discovery that Jesus' death was also of essential significance for our redemption. The intrinsic link between death and resurrection was brought out particularly strongly by St Paul (Phil 2 : 8–9). Only against the background of the resurrection, which dominated everything, could the death of Jesus also be given a meaning. St Paul did so so often and so forcibly that later generations — having lost touch with the scriptural basis — could only concentrate on the redemptive value of Jesus' death, while neglecting the resurrection.

It was only hesitantly, therefore, that believers could give a meaning to the mystery of Jesus' death. A number of these explanations were gradually worked out.[26] Thus in the oldest letter of St. Paul we can still hear an echo of the opinion that the death of Jesus was proof of the wickedness of the Jews (1 Thess 2 : 15). This apologetic perspective of the violent death of Jesus is also maintained in the ancient type of preaching of which the Acts of the Apostles gives some examples (Acts 2 : 23; 3 : 13–15; 5 : 30). The need was also felt, probably at the same time, of using the death of Jesus not merely as a counter-argument, but also as a positive factor in instruction. Studying the prophets faithfully, the first Christians discovered that the death of Jesus was "according to the Scriptures". This made it possible to give a theological meaning to the death of Jesus. It was the will of God. Jesus could have escaped such an end — "but how then should the Scriptures be fulfilled which say that it must be so?" (Mt 26 : 54.) In the pre-Pauline tradition quoted by the Apostle as he is giving his testimony to the resurrection

[26] See H.-D. Knigge, "Erlösung durch Jesu Tod", *Una Sancta* 18 (1963), pp. 151–66; O. Kuss, *Auslegung und Verkündigung* (1963), pp. 281–328.

we read the words: "that Christ died for our sins according to the Scriptures" (1 Cor 15:3). As a prelude to a systematic exposition of the Scriptures "beginning with Moses" but then touching on "all the prophets," the risen Lord says to the disciples on the road to Emmaus: "Must not the Messiah have suffered all these things, so to enter into his glory?" (Lk 24:26.) In the Gospel of St Matthew, this procedure is the key to the whole composition of the book. This perspective gave rise to an early Christology which saw the whole of Jesus' life and death as parallel to and the fulfilment of Isaiah's prophecy about the Suffering Servant of Yahweh.

Thinking of Jesus' death in the framework provided by the Old Testament, the first Christians came also to consider it as a sacrifice, in fact as a vicarious sacrifice on behalf of others. It is quite possible that the notion goes back to the preaching of Jesus himself, in so far as he revealed himself as the Suffering Servant of Yahweh of Deutero-Isaiah. In the time of the Maccabees the idea of an expiatory death on behalf of others is certainly already familiar. The Jews were already struggling with the grave problem of the violent death of men who died for their loyalty to Yahweh. There is an effort to give it a positive explanation in the prayer of the last of the Maccabean brothers before his martyrdom: "Like my brothers, I give my body and my life out of love for the laws of the fathers. And I pray God that he may speedily be gracious once more towards the people, that he may bring you through misfortune and suffering to confess that he alone is God, and that the anger of the most High, which has justly been enkindled against the whole of our people, may end with me and my brothers" (2 Macc 7:37f.). The notion that the blood of animals, offered

37

on the covering of the ark of the covenant, could bring about reconciliation and the blotting out of guilt, was much older. St Paul takes up this thought when he writes in Rom 3:25 that God "has put forward Jesus as an expiatory offering *(hilasterion)* through faith in his blood". "Hilasterion", translated here as expiatory sacrifice, means strictly speaking the covering on the ark of the covenant. Every year, on the great day of reconciliation, the blood of the sacrificial offerings was poured upon it. A similar interpretation of Jesus' death, but in a less drastic form, is found in many other places, such as the narratives of the institution of the Eucharist, where Jesus' blood is said to be "the blood of the covenant, which is poured out for many" (Mk 14:24).

It was not only to the past that primitive Christianity looked for enligthenment on the mystery of Jesus' death. The effort was made to bring out the significance of this shocking fact by drawing analogies with an everyday reality of the time, the ransom of slaves. Slaves and prisoners of war in antiquity could be set free by the payment of a ransom. This metaphor had the great advantage for the first preachers that it had, as it were, a foot in two camps. For the Jews it evoked the memory of the texts of the Bible which showed God setting Israel free from the bondage of Egypt. The pagans were reminded of the emancipation of their own slaves. Hence faith in the redemptive power of Jesus' death could be expressed by saying that he "gave his life as a ransom for many" (Mk 10:45).

A similar formula occurs frequently in the letters of St Paul. Rom 3:34 speaks of "the redemption which is in Christ Jesus". The reality which this metaphor seeks to suggest is given clear expression in Eph 1:7: "In Christ we have redemption (ransom) through his blood — the forgiveness of sins." Sometimes the notion of ransom is central: "You have been bought, at a price" (1 Cor 6 : 20). Church fathers and theologians were later to build top-heavy constructions on the substructure of this metaphor. The everyday reality which is behind it shows through very clearly at 1 Cor 7 : 22 f.: "The Christian slave is a freeman of the Lord; and he who is called as a freeman is a slave of Christ. You have been bought, at a price." In St Paul's train of thought, there is no doubt as to what we have been bought free from. It is sin. But he can also say in this connection that we have been freed from "the flesh," "the law" and above all, "death". Death always carries the stigma of sin (Rom 5:12). By freely taking upon himself human death out of obedience to the Father, Jesus has set us free from sin and death. What had once been the symbol of an absurd self-assertion (Gen 3:5) is now innerly transformed and becomes the symbol of supreme self-emptying (Phil 2 : 7–8), so that here death and resurrection go together.

A very different aspect of the same reality is expressed in St Paul's later letters in particular. Here the redemption through Jesus is interpreted by means of a Gnostic pattern of thought through which the cosmic dimensions of this redemptive act are also brought to light. Redemption is seen as the establishment of peace between Jews and Gentiles which, especially according to the Letter to the Colossians, is to have consequences throughout the whole cosmos. Through his death, Jesus has conquered the hostile powers and broken down the wall of partition. This metaphor is clearly in accordance with the Gnostic notion according to which the partition between "pneuma" and "matter" is broken down, so that the elements of spirit ("pneuma") or "light" which have been imprisoned in matter may be led back to the kingdom of spirit. The region between the two kingdoms is peopled by principalities and powers which must first be conquered if the redeemer is to make his way through. "He has disarmed the principalities and powers and made a public show of them. He has triumphed over them through the cross" (Col 2:15; cf. Eph 2:11–18; Col 1:15–20). In later Jewish-Christian speculation on the descent into hell, this theme is also brought out.[27]

It seems quite clear that what the New Testament authors had in mind throughout was what has been described above as the "objective redemption". But the most acute question which we encountered in the discussion in the previous chapter was: how does the saving work of Christ come into the life of the individual faithful? St Paul in particular is constantly pre-occupied with this question. In brief, his answer is as follows. The redemption which took place in principle in the life of Jesus comes to us through faith — our concrete *act* of faith — and the sacraments. Through faith, man goes outside himself and thus delivers himself up to another, — in the present case, to Christ, of whom it has been affirmed, in the testimonies cited above, that he took death upon himself on our behalf. Hence St Paul finds it extremely important to affirm that through faith, we have been crucified together with Christ (cf. Gal 2:19–20). This faith, like every truly human attitude, has to express itself outwardly. Certain means of expression of our faith are offered to us by the Lord himself. These are, above all, baptism and the Eucharist. When we participate in faith in

[27] See J. Daniélou, *The Theology of Jewish Christianity* (1964).

these sacraments, we enter into fellowship with the dying and rising Lord (Rom 6:3–11; 1 Cor 10:16–21). This fundamental revelation will have to be discussed later in more detail.

2. Deliverance through divinization

When men embody the vision of faith in concrete realities, the expression must naturally bear the marks of its times. Meditation on the faith and the proclamation of the faith are efforts to give it its immediate relevance. A historical event is interpreted in another historical context. We saw that in the New Testament this effort gave rise to a wide diversity in the interpretation of the redemptive act. When we look closely at this process of interpretation to which the proclamation of the faith is necessarily submitted, two conclusions follow which are of great importance. Firstly, it is a warning to us not to regard any particular historically-conditioned interpretation of the redemptive event as timeless and eternally obligatory. Believers would have been spared much uncertainty and the resulting misery if Christian preachers had been more thoroughly persuaded of this fundamental fact. Secondly, contemplation of a historically-conditioned interpretation of the redemptive event provides the possibility of finding at the present moment, in continuity with our own past, a new form of expression. Man never starts from an absolute zero either in his own individual life or in community groups. We are always to some extent definitely orientated before we take our destiny into our own hands. Knowledge of our own past at its most intimately personal helps us to come to grips with our present task. If we shake off the past under the illusion that we are making a totally new beginning, its secret revenge is all the more painful.

We have a clear example of a historically-conditioned interpretation of the redemptive event in St Irenaeus of Lyons. If we try to apply his perspective, unchanged, to our own days, there will naturally be fallacies. But if we dismiss him without more ado, we lose the change of throwing once more into relief, in our own changed conditions of existence, some valuable elements which St Irenaeus underlined in his treatment of the redemption.

A remarkable fact is apparent. St Irenaeus, writing about a hundred years later than St Paul, makes his contemplation of our redemption bear far less on the death of Jesus. It has even been possible to affirm — though not justifiably[28] — that according to St Irenaeus the death on the cross had no significance at all for our redemption. But in St Irenaeus' time the interpretations given by St Paul seem to have become the common traditional good. Hence there was no need to repeat the Pauline message in express terms. It had simply to be made relevant. St Irenaeus lived in a totally different situation which was already strongly coloured by the presence of very fantastic aberrations. Having come from Asia Minor, knowing Rome well and ruling the See of Lyons, St Irenaeus was well acquainted with the books of these fanciful authors. They roused him to anger, and though he was not naturally a publicist, as he himself confesses, he felt himself forced to write a refutation of the heresies which were cropping up around him.

[28] See G. Wingren, *Man and Incarnation* (1959), pp. 121 f., note 23.

In the first book of his *Adversus Haereses* he gives a panorama of all the strange notions which he had come across in recent times. This map of Gnosticism throws a startling light on the age. What principally dismayed the Bishop of Lyons was the licentious mode of life of many of those who proclaimed themselves to be enlightened. This dismay on a very practical level forced him to consider the principles or theories behind their behaviour. They kept to none of the precepts of the Church, had no hesitation in partaking in the sacrificial meals of heathens, enjoyed the fights between beasts in the arena and allowed themselves all sorts of freedom in sexual matters. A deacon from a Christian community in Asia, married to a woman "as stunted in mental as in bodily growth", found to his bewilderment that his wife had been seduced by one of these enlightened Gnostics.[29]

These disturbing events were the occasion for Irenaeus to investigate the spiritual background of these phenomena. Though his heavily ironical description makes the analysis difficult at times, it seems that these "heresies" were neither the result of rebelliousness nor of the search for comfort. The whole Hellenistic world was struggling with the question of salvation and redemption. Even Stoic philosophy, of which the great representative in Irenaeus' time was the Emperor Marcus Aurelius, took this problem into account. Some thinkers who had made the acquaintance of Christianity combined elements of the Christian faith with the then fashionable philosophy in the endeavour to reach a workable philosophy of life. The problem of evil was naturally of primary importance. The most

[29] St Irenaeus, *Libri quinque adversus haereses*, ed. by W. W. Harvey (1857), 2 vols. (reprint 1965), Bk. I, ch. 13, no. 5.

43

obvious way to explain it was to take refuge in a "dualism". When there is not one but two or more ultimate principles to explain everything which happens on earth, evil and suffering can be always made intelligible. A Gnostic called Valentinus, who is often quoted by Irenaeus, had evolved an ingenious doctrine according to which the eternal good God and the principle of the material, evil world were radically distinct. Practically the whole of sacred Scripture was re-interpreted in terms of this fundamental *a priori*. Irenaeus gives many examples. Since such interpretations were linked up with a fashionable philosophy they found wide and ready acceptance. In this way a great deal of wordy nonsense was talked, alongside of the serious discussions of fundamentals. Many Christians were intimidated. This happened still more frequently when people began to count on their inferiority complexes. Those who did not fall in with the current fashion were accused contemptuously of being "idiots" (*Adversus Haereses,* I, 6, 4). Those who accepted the esoteric doctrines were given to understand that they belonged to the elect who can never perish. Since they are animated by the good principle, they can do whatever they want to (*Adversus Haereses,* I, 6, 2). St Irenaeus tried to put an end to the resulting confusion by means of a book which would lay bare the dubious origins of these theories and practices. The true faith has its origin not in private and secret revelations but in the public preaching of the Church. This preaching, concentrated in the hands of the bishops as the heads of the local worshipping communities, can be traced and checked back to the first preaching of the Apostles (tradition).

Meant originally as a brief polemical writing to unmask the

wiles of error, the *Adversus Haereses* grew into a work in five parts which is hardly distinguished by a strict structural principle. Nonetheless, the thought of St Irenaeus is constantly inspired by an idea which is expressed again and again, that of the "recapitulation" of all creation under the one Head, Christ. Against his adversaries, St Irenaeus re-affirms for his faithful that the one God has reconciled all things and all men in Christ. No one is good or evil by nature, elect or reprobate, but all mankind is called in Christ to participate in the divine nature. If the redemptive death of Christ on the cross is not given great prominence by St Irenaeus,[30] this is due to the fact that he attributes decisive significance to the *incarnation* of the Son of God. The incarnation was a concrete historical event which included no doubt the death on the cross, but which embraced in fact the whole of a human life. God became man in Christ in order that man should be divinized.[31] The contemporaries of St Irenaeus, unlike ourselves, were accustomed to think of the human race as a concrete unity. Hence the sin of Adam could be regarded as destructive for the whole human race. If one member of the human race succeeded in overcoming from within the sin which had perverted the whole race, this redemption naturally had repercussions on the race of man as a whole.

It is of supreme importance not to underestimate the social dimensions which are here attributed to sin as well as to redemption. We have been accustomed far too long to consider both sin and salvation as highly individual events which are played out purely and simply in the individual relationship between "my soul" and God. And hence when St Irenaeus' doctrine of re-

[30] N. Bonwetsch, *Die Theologie des heiligen Irenäus* (1925), p. 113.
[31] *Adversus Haereses*, IV, 33, 4; III, 19, 1; V, prologue.

demption was re-discovered, it came in for criticism at once.
It seemed that the ethical and personal categories were neglected
in his theology. Instead of sin and forgiveness, he mostly speaks
of death or corruption and life or immortality. One could get
the impression of a sort of mechanical process, as if something
had been "physically" altered in humanity through the incarnation. The incarnation seemed to have launched a sort of
automatic process of divinization.

This interpretation, which has constantly been recurring since
Harnack,[32] fails to do justice to the Bishop of Lyons. Though
redemption, conceived as the "divinization" of the human race,
does not in fact answer *our* questions — what is the relationship of the individual to mankind as a whole? — nonetheless,
our eyes are opened to the fact that the redemption through
Christ has brought about a new situation for the whole of mankind. Further, when using his "physical" terminology, St
Irenaeus means something much more than is often too quickly
assumed. When he speaks of "death," he means "separation
from God". Life is "fellowship with God" (*Adversus Haereses*,
V, 27, 2), or more precisely, "obedience to God" (*Adversus
Haereses*, IV, 39, 1). The agreement is so striking between the
train of thought and combination of ideas in the doctrine of
St Irenaeus and in what St Paul says in the sixth chapter of his
Letter to the Romans or in 1 Cor 15 : 53–58, that one must
either accuse St Paul of thinking in "physical" terms, or give
an explicitly religious interpretation to the terms which seem
at any rate to have a physical connotation in both.

According to St Irenaeus, the Word of God, at his incarnation, took upon himself the life of man which had been per-

[32] See J. Gross, *Entstehungsgeschichte des Erbsündendogmas* (1960), p. 87.

verted by sin. Guided throughout his whole life by obedience to the Father, Jesus then conquered sin (*Adversus Haereses*, V, 19, 1). "Man is taken up into the triumph, the fulfilment, the resurrection and the ascension. ... This Son of the Virgin Mary, God with us, descended to the depths of the earth to seek the lost sheep and to offer man when he had found him to the eternal Father. In him the Father produced the first-fruits of the resurrection. Hence just as the head is risen from the dead, so too the rest of the body will rise, that is, all men, who will be given life when they have passed the time of their condemnation for disobedience. ... There are many mansions in my Father's house, just as there are many members in the Body" (*Adversus Haereses*, III, 19, 3). The question which interests us here is whether St Irenaeus did really think of redemption as a process in which we were included in the humanity of Jesus and hence more or less automatically redeemed. This would in fact be a very weak position to take up against the Gnostics whom he was opposing. And it is quite clear that according to St Irenaeus man must explicitly insert himself into the humanity of Jesus by personal acts. This is done above all by faith and the sacraments. Man is only a "living man" when he "believes in the coming of the Son of God and establishes the Spirit of God in his heart by this faith. Only he who does this is rightly called a man ... and living" (*Adversus Haereses*, V, 9, 2). St Irenaeus affirms with astonishing clarity that faith must be a free human act (*Adversus Haereses*, IV, 37, 5). There is no question of an automatic redemption. Baptism and the Eucharist are also of essential importance to St Irenaeus. Having repeated the well-known metaphor of the many grains of wheat which become one bread, he notes that before the grains of wheat can be made into one bread water and fire are also necessary. So too with us when we wish to become one in Christ. "Our bodies are united by the bath of incorruption, our spirits are united by the Holy Spirit" (*Adversus Haereses*, III, 17, 2). He says of the Eucharist: "When our bodies receive the Eucharist, they are no longer subject to corruption but have the hope of the resurrection" (*Adversus Haereses*, IV, 18, 5; V, 2, 2 and 3).[33]

In St Irenaeus' concept of redemption there is still another element which needs to be stressed. The real author of man's redemption is God himself. The one God and Father sent his Son in sinful flesh to reconcile his creation to himself. In Christ, the second Adam, God's original plan of creation is taken up again. St Irenaeus says very clearly that man is impotent to redeem himself. If someone else in the strict sense does not redeem us, we remain captive to our illusions. "Man who had fallen into bondage is freed by the mercy of God the Father, who had pity on his creature. He gave him redemption through his Word, that is, he renewed him through Christ so that man might learn experimentally that he attains eternal life not through his own strength but through God's grace" (*Adversus Haereses*, V, 21, 3). If one pursues this thought to the conclusion that man is deprived of all power of being active in the work of redemption,[34] one falls victim to the schema of mutual competition which has been described above. Further, one would fail to recognize the role which St Irenaeus very clearly accords to the humanity of Christ in the work of redemption.

[33] See V. Palashovsky, "La théologie eucharistique de S. Irénée", *Studia Patristica*, vol. II, part 2 (1957), pp. 277–81.
[34] G. Aulén, *Christus Victor* (9th ed., 1965), pp. 28–35.

Man is not degraded into a passive, mindless object but is inserted precisely as a free agent into God's plan of salvation. The mystery of God is embodied in Christ's free offering of himself. In a passage which contains elements of another theme which we shall discuss in the next section, St Irenaeus declares roundly: "If it were not a man who overcame the enemy, he would not be justly conquered. But on the other hand, if God had not freely bestowed salvation, man would not have attained it in triumph. If God and man were not united, man would not have been able to participate in immortality" (*Adversus Haereses*, III, 18, 7).

St Irenaeus' teaching on redemption bears unmistakably the signs of his times. He proves thereby that he understood that his task was to proclaim the faith to men of flesh and blood. To refute the menacing dualism of the Gnostics, he reduces the whole of human history, including the Fall and the redemption, to one event in which creation and new creation are interwoven with one another. When he appeals in this process to the organic unity of the human race, we find this difficult to understand — unless we are fervent adherents of Teilhard de Chardin. It is nonetheless made clear that sin and redemption are not strictly individual events but have a social dimension. In the restoration of fellowship God takes the initiative. But since he is the transcendent principle, he essentially includes the proper activity of man and does not rule it out.

3. Justice takes its course

Since St Irenaeus was Bishop of Lyons, the map of Europe has undergone drastic changes. Behind these changes there are cultural ones of a profound nature. It is not then astonishing that a believer of the eleventh century, travelling through wide regions of what is now Italy, France and England, should have naturally brought with him a different notion of redemption. St Anselm of Canterbury, though just as much inspired by sacred Scripture as St Irenaeus, had a totally different perspective. The death of Christ on the cross is heavily stressed and the new life of the resurrection comes less specifically to the fore.

Anselm was born in Aosta about 1033. In consequence of a sharp disagreement with his father, he left his native Burgundian land. After about three years of wandering, he settled down for a time in Normandy and entered the monastery of Bec, at the instigation of his fellow-countryman, the Abbot Lanfranc. This monastery, founded by William the Conqueror, kept up lively relations through its founder with the newly-conquered country on the far side of the Channel. Lanfranc was installed by his king as Archbishop of Canterbury, and Anselm became his successor there. He was then sixty years of age, but the most turbulent part of his life was still before him. The historical bonds between Church and State, exemplified in Lanfranc and William the Conqueror, were secretly charged with a high tension of explosive force. The investiture strife, in which Anselm was directly involved, was one of the consequences. The Archbishop of Canterbury was forced several times to take refuge in exile, and his search for help took him to Rome. On his travels, he completed in great haste his *Cur Deus Homo,* since portions of it had already been copied by others without his knowledge.

Thus the monk Anselm was a much travelled man who was well in touch with the times he lived in. He knew what was happening in Europe. His theology and the subconscious patterns of his thought are marked by his experience. His notion of God displays features of the feudal lord who maintains his rights according to strict rules. In his picture of Christ, the tranquil figure of the Roman crucifix begins to make way for the suffering man of Gothic art. And there had also been great changes in the ordinary life of the Church.[35] While for the first generation of Christians baptism was the great and unrepeatable event in which the definitive change of heart and life took place, the sacrament of penance had gradually come to receive more attention. The penances to be imposed were codified in penitentials. Notable changes had taken place in the attitude towards the Eucharist, inspired to some extent by recent polemics in which Anselm's greatly revered master Lanfranc had taken part. From this period onward, the great stress was on the real, almost "physical" presence of Christ. The frequent celebration of the Eucharist in the monasteries came to be less and less community celebrations. The aspect of individual union with Christ came more strongly into the foreground.

Anselm's view of the redemption is clearly marked by all these circumstances. And this is so clearly so that authors for whom the Middle Ages represent the gloomy nadir of European history have not one good word to say for Anselm's soteriology. After Ritschl and Harnack, a number of Scandinavian authors in particular have gone to extremes in their criticism of Anselm, hoping to free the Reformation notion of the redemption from foreign accretions.[36] They saw in Anselm the

[35] G. Hunston Williams, "The Sacramental Presuppositions of Anselm's *Cur Deus Homo*", *Church History* 26 (1957), pp. 245–74.
[36] G. Aulén, *Christus Victor* (1965); O. Tiililä, *Das Strafleiden Christi* (1941), Criticism in H. Alpers, *Die Versöhnung durch Christus. Zur Typologie der Schule von Lund* (1964); J. McIntyre, *St Anselm and his Critics* (1954).

great representative of what was called the "Latin type" of soteriology. The ingredients of it are supposed to be found as early as the juridically-minded Tertullian and Cyprian. Anselm then pursued this line of thought to its logical conclusion, so that all his thinking was focused on the principle that satisfaction must be made for sin according to the laws of justice. He is reproached above all with maintaining that man had to accomplish something of value to God. Hence God would no longer be the sole author of our redemption and man would have an effective share in his own redemption. There would be a sort of juridical transaction between two equal partners, by virtue of which God would be obliged to bestow forgiveness on man. Christ would only have come in order to make satisfaction to the divine majesty whose justice had been offended.

This account of Anselm's position is one-sided. It is true that justice plays a large role in his thought. And it cannot be denied that the feudalism of the Middle Ages made a strong contribution to his thought at this point. But it must not be forgotten that the traditional line of thought from the Bible to St Augustine provided Anselm with a train of thought in which the justice of God plays an important role.[37] All the extrinsic and juridical elements in justice are greatly modified thereby, as we shall see.

What was Anselm's argument? It is noticeable, first of all, that he definitely rejects one of the images which we were able to point to in sacred Scripture. Anselm refuses under any condition to regard redemption as a sort of ransom. The reason for this deliberate rejection is to be found in the heights of spec-

[37] See J. Plagnieux, "Le binôme *iustitia — potentia* dans la sotériologie augustinienne et anselmienne", *Spicilegium Beccense,* I (1959), pp. 141–54.

ulation which theology had reached on this matter. Many Fathers of the Church had gone so far in this direction that they regarded Christ as the ransom which had to be paid to the devil. Briefly and firmly, Anselm dismisses this notion which was well rooted in a venerable tradition. The devil, he said, had no rights with regard to God.[38] Anselm's own conception was based on a different principle. "He who does not give God the honour which is his due, withholds from him what is his own and dishonours him. And this is sin. As long as he has not given back what he has robbed, he remains in debt. And it is not sufficient merely to give back what he has robbed. For the insult which he has offered, man must give more than he robbed" (*Cur Deus Homo*, I, 11). With this starting-point of Anselm, we are in a different world from that of Irenaeus. The juridical relationships of feudalism made the monk of Bec sensitive to the theme of "justice", which also echoes in sacred Scripture. Jesus pays with his blood the price which justice demands in satisfaction for our sins. By placing this theme in the foreground, Anselm could make the redemption a highly relevant and appealing reality for the men of his time. He then goes on, with an almost painfully strict logic, to argue that man can do nothing with regard to God except what he is already obliged to do anyway. Thus there can never be a surplus. Hence real satisfaction can only be made by a God-man. Satisfaction can only be made "when someone pays God for the sin of man something that is of more value than all that is outside God. Further, he must be able to give God something of his own which surpasses all that exists outside God, he must himself be

---

[38] *Cur Deus Homo*, I, 7 (E. T., London, 1886 ff.); cf. R. Rogues, *Pourquoi Dieu s'est fait homme* (French tr., introduction and commentary, 1963).

greater than all that exists outside God. Hence only God can effect this satisfaction. On the other hand, only man must do it, otherwise man does not make satisfaction" (*Cur Deus Homo*, II, 6).

Thus the question of "why God became man", a question which stirred up much feeling in medieval disputes between Jews and Christians,[39] is on the way to being answered by a strictly logical piece of reasoning. But there remained still deeper problems. One of these which had already been felt acutely by the first Christians, as we have seen above, was: why had the God-man to die such a shameful death?

Anselm starts to reason things out again. He does not argue like an outsider who is trying to come to the faith by the use of logic. From within the faith, he tries to come to a sure answer by means of reasoning. The God-man, he argues, was undoubtedly mortal, but being himself absolutely sinless, he did not merit death. Like every other creature, he was undoubtedly bound to absolute obedience to God. By giving his life freely up to God, therefore, Christ did more than he was obliged to as regards God. The Father then bestows his reward on the Son for this voluntary, non-obligatory death. But God the Father can bestow nothing on the Son which is not already his by right. Hence the reward given in return must be given to others — to those to whom the Son wills to pass on his own reward.

Sin demands satisfaction. If this is not made, justice is not done. This theme of "justice" dominates the whole argument of Anselm. Nonetheless, he knows that God and man are not

[39] See P. van der Plaas, "Des hl. Anselms 'Cur Deus Homo' auf dem Boden der jüdisch-christlichen Polemik des Mittelalters", *Divus Thomas* (Freiburg) 17 (1929), pp. 446–67; 18 (1930), pp. 18–32.

on equal terms and hence that there can be no question of
strict justice. Why then does he come to such daring conclusions,
as they seem to us as we look on from outside? Anselm,
however, could be more at ease in dealing with this theme; it
did not have the same awkward implications for him which it
has for us. At present, law, the juridical mentality and everything
connected with this sphere are almost synonymous with arbitrary rules of the game and not at all determinations which
flow from the nature of things themselves. From this modern
point of view, it may be true to say that to let justice take its
course is often the supreme injustice — *summum ius, summa
iniuria.* But the very fact of using this standard expression
shows that one recognizes that there is another concept of justice
and law which is far from arbitrary. If one pursues this line of
thought, one finds that Anselm's view is based on a profound
and valuable truth, the presence of which has not been hitherto
sufficiently recognized and respected. His notion of "justice"
is closer to the biblical view than later historians give us to
understand.[40] Anselm maintains vigorously that justice is the
very nature of God. The fact that he commands something is
not precisely what makes it good and just. If that were so, God
could ordain in a fully arbitrary way that murder or lying was
good and just. But the contrary is true. It is because something
is intrinsically good and just that God can command it (*Cur
Deus Homo*, I, 12, 13). Hence laws and precepts are not arbitrary commandments but the imperative which is given with
the truth that God is God. So too sin is not the transgression of
an arbitrary precept, to which then a further arbitrary demand

[40] See E. R. Fairweather, "Iustitia Dei as the Ratio of the Incarnation",
Spicilegium Beccense, I (1959), pp. 327–35.

for satisfaction is appended. It is an infraction of the "ordo debitus," the order of things such as it intrinsically is by virtue of the nature of God himself and of his creation. By infringing the order, man does injury to himself, not to God. "No one can honour or dishonour God, in so far as God himself is concerned" (*Cur Deus Homo*, I, 15). Hence satisfaction for sin is not an extrinsic demand for a restoration of honour of which the divine majesty has been deprived. To be able to make satisfaction is a glimpse of God's mercy, which enables man to repair the harm done to himself.

It is clear, therefore, that whenever Anselm speaks of the crucifixion of Christ as "satisfaction", he is undoubtedly well aware that he is using a metaphor. It is not a matter of paying a sort of "damages" which have been assessed quite arbitrarily for the disturbance of the order of justice. In that case, the death of Jesus would have been a fine for a traffic offence: the lightness or heaviness of the fine depends on the laws passed by a body of legislators and the verdict passed by the magistrate in court. Like Irenaeus, Anselm regards the death of Jesus as a free act of supreme obedience (*Cur Deus Homo*, II, 18). This freely-accepted death is not the payment of an extrinsic price for sin, with God binding himself arbitrarily to bestow redemption in exchange. The death of Christ is intrinsically the restoration of the divine order on the human level. The divine order had been violated on the human level by the disobedience of sin. Hence the restoration naturally means free obedience.

The preceding considerations make it clear that Anselm is rejecting a notion of redemption or ransom as imposed by tradition. It was a notion which had obviously had its day and was in fact now apt to evoke unavoidable misunderstandings. Hence Anselm resolutely makes use of his freedom to tell the Gospel message in another way to his contemporaries.

It is very noticeable here that Anselm is profoundly filled by the conviction that man cannot redeem himself. What man has violated by sin has an other-worldly dimension. This dimension of the "wholly other", called God by Anselm, is clearly something which he finds absolutely obvious. This is a clear proof that his starting-point is that of faith. At the same time he is also fully convinced that if redemption is to be a human reality, it will also demand some effort from man himself. These two elements are elaborated by concentrating the discussion on the truth that Jesus is both God and man. How the redemption brought about by the God-man (the "objective" redemption) comes to be applied to us is not specifically discussed by Anselm. It may well be that he took the sacramental presence of Jesus in the Eucharist so much for granted that he did not find it necessary to go into the notion of "subjective" redemption.

Anselm has also been reproached with laying so much emphasis on the free self-dedication and obedience of the man Jesus that the divine initiative in the redemption is in danger of being lost sight of.

This accusation reveals once more how strongly people are influenced by the schema of competition, God versus man, which is so constant a threat. The Godhead and humanity are never competitors, least of all in the God-man Jesus. We must not think that when something is ascribed to the human activity of Jesus, this must be registered as a sort of loss to his Godhead. This kind of thinking obviously tries to divide up Jesus "horizontally" into two parts, one human and one divine. But if divinity and humanity — above all in Jesus — are regarded "vertically", the divinity is the dimension in depth of Jesus' humanity, while his humanity is the manifestation or interpretation of the transcendence of God on the earthly plane.

The influence of Anselm's views on the redemption was extraordinarily strong. He had obviously succeeded in expressing this mystery in a way which touched profoundly the heart of medieval man. But it would be wrong to assume that all theologians then followed Anselm uncritically. Thomas Aquinas in particular, who lived two centuries later than Anselm, displays a sound sense of the relativity of all theological systems. His criticism is gentle — so gentle, in fact, that even the modern reader is in danger of overlooking the implicit corrections and changes of direction which it contains. As is well known, Aquinas was not inclined to make frontal assaults on settled opinions. But in his own rather subtle way, he constantly disassociates himself from standard views, by saving elegantly the authority of the person who introduced a given opinion while at the same time filling the kernel of the opinion with a totally new content. Two elements are at once noticeable in his treatment of the redemption. Firstly, it is clear that he is prepared to interpret the mystery of our redemption very expressly in several different ways, which have no apparent connection with one another. He demonstrates that Christ *merited* redemption for us, that his passion and death made *satisfaction* for sin, that the crucifixion redeemed us because it was a *sacrifice*. Full justice is also done to the scriptural notion of redemption as a *ransom*, and the discussion ends with a picture of the redemption as taking place through a sacramentally real contact with Christ.[41]

[41] *Summa Theologica*, III, q. 48.

When these texts are examined more closely, a second element, more difficult to determine, shows itself behind this series of themes. Each particular aspect of the mystery of our redemption as presented by Thomas Aquinas is simply one of the many possible images which can be used to portray the reality of it. Throughout these metaphors he gives as it were incidentally a number of directives for a very realistic *sacramental* notion of our redemption. These may be summed up as follows.

During his earthly life, Jesus followed out in an absolutely unique and perfect way the will of the Father. By this fundamental obedience, this inward self-dedication,[42] Jesus attacked the principle of sin, the effort of self-assertion and self-assurance. Thus he "merited" for himself his glorification.[43] What Thomas Aquinas means by this is that like all human acts, the human acts of Jesus had an intrinsic proportion to *his* future. Good and evil have at once their own intrinsic sanction in my future. Thus the actual end of Jesus' life by which he put the seal on his constant self-renunciation was the absolute affirmation of the Other, the Father. But during his earthly life Jesus performed and explained before his disciples a number of symbolic acts, especially at the Last Supper, whereby they were to make present once more to future believers the reality of his life and death. He was to remain present in such acts. When his life and death were proclaimed during the celebration of these acts, believers were to be summoned to accept these expressions of Jesus' obedience as manifestations of their own personal readiness for self-dedication. Thus they were to confess their faith in a concrete way, in the sacraments. By forming a true fellowship in the worship of the Church, they too, in the power

[42] *Ibid.*, q. 47, a. 2.   [43] *Ibid.*, q. 19, a. 3 and 4.

of Christ, were to overcome the root of sin, the barricades of egoism. No fellowship is ever possible without the grace of a certain form of self-renunciation, without which there can be no affirmation of the other. This selfless affirmation of the other is faith. Wherever fellowship — *communio* — comes about in Christ's name and in the form commanded by him, the *excommunicatio* — sin — is destroyed. Hence, according to Thomas, redemption is accomplished "through faith in the sacraments of faith".[44] Faith is the actual affirmation of the other, and the sacraments are the ecclesial expression of this affirmation by which the fellowship is constituted. This truth must now be more fully developed.[45]

[44] *Ibid.*, q. 48, a. 2, ad 2.
[45] For a technical discussion of the views of St Thomas, see B. A. Willems in *Tijdschrift voor Theologie* 5 (1965), esp. pp. 42–47.

III

THE FELLOWSHIP
OF THE CHURCH AS REDEMPTION

1. Eucharistic presence

God, the mysterious Other, redeems us through Christ. Both Irenaeus and Anselm were profoundly convinced of this truth. But the questions with which we found ourselves confronted in our first chapter were not explicitly posed by these writers. One of the first and most acute questions was: how does the encounter with the redeeming figure from the past take place now? Christ died, and "a cloud took him out of (our) sight" (cf. Acts 1:9). During the twenty centuries which have passed since then a huge mass of clouds has built up. Those who have seen the history of Christendom as an obstacle which prevents them from coming into contact with Christ, are not lying in this regard. Dostoievsky has given classical expression to this view in the legend of the Grand Inquisitor. But even when this difficulty is resolved, there is still another problem and one to which we have now become particularly sensitive. If it is in fact possible to encounter the redeemer in the present day, must he not then completely absorb our attention and turn it away from our fellow-men? This has in fact happened, and the phenomenon has been acutely observed.[46] There have been Christians who felt themselves inspired by their faith in Christ to correct those who were still awaiting the Messiah. Hostility towards the Jews, where it occurred in the Middle Ages, could be traced to a conviction that it was blasphemous still to be awaiting "him who comes" after Jesus Christ had come. It is a commonplace among modern critics of Christianity that Christians are so preoccupied with being a Church that they forget to help their needy fellowmen. This is a phenomenon which has many very real ramifications in ordinary life. There has been and still is a sort of pietist mysticism which seeks Christ in withdrawal and isolation, without the proper safeguards and motivations. There has been and still is a nervous, dogmatic concentration on Christ which looks on the duties of everyday life as a loss and distraction. And had the devotion to the Eucharist which was so marked a feature of Catholic life till recently really much effect on the everyday life which began "again" at the end of Sunday mass?

Neither Irenaeus nor Anselm discussed such questions with such interest as is accorded them at present. Nonetheless, they were concerned with them implicitly. The pastoral interests of their writings enabled them to hold fast, as though by intuition, to the basic conviction that the role of God, Christ *and of us men* must be safeguarded in the discussion of redemption. This is what gave rise to the rhetorical question of Anselm: could not God in his omnipotence have wrought the redemption in another way, without the cruelty in which it was actually accomplished? And his answer accordingly was: No, man had

[46] D. Sölle, *Christ the Representative: An Essay in Theology after the 'Death of God'* (1967).

to take part, by freely delivering himself up to death. This is why redemption was accomplished by a God-*man*. Irenaeus solved the problem by making the humanity of Christ part of the unity of the human race, so that we too were inserted into the redemptive work of Christ. The validity of this doctrine of Irenaeus is still argued for at the present day.[47] The dogmatics of the Reformation in particular reproached both Anselm and Irenaeus with denying the truth that God is the sole author of redemption.[48] But the reproach is an unreal one. In point of fact, the great merit of the two writers is that they did not fall victim to the notion of "competition" which is obviously at the base of the accusation.

Though of course the terms "objective" and "subjective" redemption do not occur in either Irenaeus or Anselm, they saw well enough the problem of interpretation which is posed by these terms. If the "subjective" redemption is eliminated out of a short-sighted fear of not doing justice to the "objective" redemption by God or Christ, then, even when inspired by highly orthodox intentions, one reduces Christianity to the caricature which cannot but be the defenceless target of the criticisms cited above. The objection is sometimes made that if the historical deed of Christ is in fact fully definitive, Christians can sit down and fold their arms and let the world go on being the world. And the same critics go a step further. The Catholic notion of the Eucharist is precisely the re-affirmation of this definitive character of Christ's sacrifice on the cross. All

---

[47] See A. Bsteh, *Zur Frage nach der Universalität der Erlösung* (1966). But his interpretation leaves unexplained the opposition of Irenaeus to the "automatic" salvation of the Gnostics.

[48] G. Aulén, *op. cit.*, pp. 84–92; A. Benoit, *Saint Irénée* (1960), pp. 229–33.

believers have to do, it seems, is simply to make present once more this definitive act. — The objection does in fact point in the correct direction, but its actual form betrays a very narrow outlook as regards the Eucharist. To explain what we mean, we shall take up again the question put above: can Christ still be encountered today?

It is a well-known fact that some men are discovered only after their death. Attention was only called to their person by the writings, the works of art or the inspired institutions which they left after them. The biography of Shakespeare must be left unwritten because we can only guess who he was and where he lived. Kierkegaard died in poverty and isolation. He was only discovered through his writings long after his death. Vincent van Gogh shared the lot of many artists of genius. It was only with the passage of time that his paintings came to be noticed, and then also his letters. This list of late starters for immortality could obviously be easily lengthened. What was common to them all was that they survived in their works. Or rather, their most profound inspiration, the spirit which animated their life and work was only recognized in what they left to us after their death. In this context, it is possible to envisage anew the possibility *for us* of coming in contact with Jesus and his Spirit. According to teaching of Scripture, it was his will that we should be constantly reminded of him. It was for this reason that he ordered the continual repetition of a gesture performed by him at the greatest hour of his life. "On the night when he was betrayed the Lord Jesus took bread, and when he had given thanks, he broke it, and said, 'This is my body which is for you. Do this in remembrance of me'" (1 Cor 11 : 23–24). The gesture was repeated after the supper, this time with the wine. "This cup is the new covenant in my blood. Do this, as often as you drink it, in remembrance of me" (v. 25). Shortly before Jesus sealed his obedience to the Father with his blood, he identified himself with a simple gift which he left to us. He willed to live on in these gifts, to remain present among us. This is a human way of acting which we encounter often enough. Someone wants to give himself to us. In order to do so, he makes use of an earthly reality which remains on the one hand ("physically") what it was, but on the other hand now participates in the person of the giver. He gives himself in the gift. Scientifically, the gift is not changed. A microscopic examination would not disclose the given in the gift. But he who believes in the love of the other has no need of such an examination. He is sure of his facts. His faith discloses to him a dimension of the proffered reality which no laboratory could show him.

Thus for the believer, an encounter with the redeeming Christ is still possible today. Each time the Eucharist is celebrated, his gesture and his words are repeated in memory of him. In his gift, accompanied by his words, the Lord himself is present among us. But the question is whether this way of looking at things does not bring up the second difficulty signalled above in all its acuteness. If Christ himself is "really present", then obviously all attention is concentrated on him. Then redemption can be understood in a very individualistic way as our dedication of ourselves to the other who appears here and now in Christ, and not as dedication to the Christ who appears to us in the other. However, the manner in which Christ wills to be present among us runs counter to such an interpretation. What we call "the Last Supper" was a gesture of Jesus which was an anticipation of the coming events. [49] He was prepared to go to the utmost extreme to show his inward self-renunciation and his dedication to the Father. This was to be manifested in his bodily death. At the meal with his disciples, Jesus anticipated in a symbolic manner his sacrificial death. Hence he offered the body which was ready for death and the blood which sealed the covenant to his fellow-guests, so that they too could offer along with him the sacrifice of the new covenant. Since the gesture took the form of a repast, the disciples were summoned to fellowship, *communio*. For the first generation of Christians the "breaking of bread" was a tangible form of mutual fellowship. [50] Through this mutual fellowship the fellowship with the redeemer became real and thus the redemption was realized. We must try to bring home to ourselves the full implications of this truth. The meaning and purpose of the real presence of Christ in his Eucharist is only seen when those who take part in the meal also form among themselves the one body of Christ. "The bread which we break, is it not a participation in the body of Christ? Because there is one loaf, we who are many are one body, for we all partake of the same loaf" (1 Cor 10:16f.; cf. 12:27). For a truly "realist" view of what we call the real presence of the Lord it is of vital importance to remember that originally the expression "body of Christ" meant the fellowship of the Church as well as the Eucharistic gifts. Thus a celebration of the Eucharist at which the community was not present seemed inconceivable to Cyprian. [51] The separation between the "real

---

[49] See J. Dupont, "'Ceci est mon corps', 'ceci est mon sang'", *Nouvelle Revue Théologique* 80 (1958), pp. 1025–41.

[50] See Acts 2:42 with variant readings.   [51] Migne, *PL*, IV, col. 386.

body of the Lord" — meaning the Eucharist — and the "mystical body of the Lord" — meaning the Church, is a highly questionable impoverishment of a way of speaking which was originally much more pregnant with meaning.[52]

There should therefore be no question of such an individualistic Eucharistic piety as is sometimes envisaged. The redemptive encounter with the Other in Christ is only real when we are ready for genuine fellowship. The prerequisite for this is that we should cease to regard ourselves as the single centre of attention. In the Eucharist, the ritual external process is that of a common meal. In the ritual form of the Eucharist in each age this must be realistically brought out. When the celebration does not succeed in inspiring those present with a concrete sense of unity and mutual service it is fundamentally deficient. The only way to supplement this deficiency is to make the theological meaning of the Eucharist go hand in hand with artistically competent efforts to give expression to the modern sense of fellowship. If this is not done, the congregation of the faithful gathered together for the Eucharist will rather feel that they have been reduced to a meagre form of ritual existence than that they have been enabled to experience a more intense form of fellowship. What is mostly at fault here is not the theology but a lack of imagination and artistic ability, since a real sense of life as it is lived today is lacking and hence no adequate form of the celebration of the Eucharist is produced.

It should also be clear that a celebration of the Eucharist which really appeals to a strong and fundamental readiness for fellowship cannot in fact be restricted to half an hour or so.

[52] H. de Lubac, *Corpus Mysticum* (2nd ed., 1949).

There must be some prelude to it in daily life, and it must have a number of consequences. If it remains a brief emotional experience without real depth, we have not penetrated to the meaning of the Eucharist. If we have been touched in the depths of our heart we shall then be moved to remember, for instance, the words of Jesus, "If you are offering your gift at the altar, and there remember that your brother has something against you, leave your gift there before the altar and go; first be reconciled to your brother and then come and offer your gift" (Mt 5:23–24).

The consequences are far-reaching. In our own times, now that the problems of community life are growing greater and greater and are brought more clearly home to the individual responsibility, this way of thinking can be the inspiration of a very comprehensive self-dedication to "the others". To be redeemed means to take others seriously, to try skilfully to ease their earthly burdens, to help them to attain their hopes, desires and joys. "Salvation" and redemption only take place when Christians are making serious and concrete efforts to renounce themselves. The Eucharist can be a centre from which helpfulness extends in ever greater circles. Thus the redemption takes place in a very concrete way in our turning away from our egoism and throwing our hearts open to one another. For the Christian, the eucharistic celebration is the prototype, but this is only the centre of a much wider transubstantiation which takes in his whole world. This cannot be brought about without what Scripture calls *metanoia*, a change of heart. The real meaning of this term can be rendered in many ways. It may be identified with "faith" (cf. Acts 20:21), and then it means that we turn towards the mystery of our fellow-men in whom we sense the manifestation of the transcendent God. Faith means that we no longer go by what is experimentally verifiable or measurably useful. This leaves the believer in a certain sense defenceless. He cannot give conclusive arguments for his self-dedication. He has undertaken a venture. Hence faith is not merely accepting a truth on authority but accepting the other as the other, taking the risk of inviting the other, without doing violence to him, to enter into one's own life. As has already been said, this means that we must die to some of the security of our ego on the superficial level. But through this death we rise to a better life, the life of the redeemed.

This is rather dramatically put — but sometimes in fact something rather dramatic is called for. More often, fundamentally the same action takes place on a more modest scale. Faith has not to express itself merely in mighty deeds of heaven-storming renunciation, but also in a simple gesture, a patient hearing, the difficult preparation for learning to listen skilfully. But the works of faith go farther afield. The desire to give other men a place in society worthy of their human dignity can impel us to responsible political action, to well-considered and careful interest in the social und economic problems of the day, in a word, to every effort whereby the believer, who knows that the world is to be made a better place for men to live in, tries to make his faith in the mystery of the other real thing.

2. The Church as event

With what has been said in the previous section we have already equivalently given a description of what the Church really is according to its most profound reality. The Church is not a statistical quantity but an event. It is not an event which comes upon us and then leaves us untouched, but an event in which we ourselves always take part. On the one hand, an other than ourselves comes upon us to offer to take us out of our egoism and set up "fellowship". This is a gift from elsewhere, dependent on the free act of another which is not within our power. As the tax-collector Matthew sat peacefully in his toll-booth, the call of Jesus, "Follow me!", came to him as a complete surprise. On the other hand, this summons calls for our active response. Fellowship cannot be formed one-sidedly. Matthew could have continued to sit at his counter and let Jesus' call to follow him go unheeded. Where one gives himself the other must accept him in faith and trust if there is really to be fellowship. The actual realization of the redemptive fellowship in the name of Christ is the Church. And hence it is present for us in its most concentrated form in the Eucharist, where we are also enabled to receive Christ's gift of himself. In face of the summons which goes forth from Jesus' words (in the preaching) and deed (in the Eucharist), we remain free. If we accept, it can only be in an act of faith. We open our hearts in order to enter into fellowship with *his* Spirit, who comes to us through words and deed. In the concrete, this comes down to the fact that his Spirit animates us to live for others like him. The "others" who first come in question are those who celebrate the Eucharist along with us. Hence when we hear the word "Church," the first thing we should think of is not the world-wide institution, but the local fellowship in the Eucharist.

The result of fellowship being set up in this way is that it is constantly being re-affirmed. Fellowship is not the sum of

individuals but a new mutual unity between men as they identify themselves with the Christ who willed to set up this community. Hence it is more than a pious metaphor when St Paul
speaks of the "body of Christ". This expression may possibly
have become trite for us, but it is really very pregnant. For a
re-appraisal of its meaning, it will be well to let ourselves feel
the impact of the background and gradual development of
Paul's doctrine of the "body of Christ". We must go back many
years before the birth of Christ. Livy tells us that the Roman
plebs were once in revolt against the patricians.[53] The consul
Menenius Agrippa sought to calm the unrest by recounting a
sort of fable — which has become famous in world literature
since Shakespeare put the story into the first act of his "Corio-
lanus". The philosopher-statesman there addresses the jeering
citizens as follow:

> There was a time when all the body's members
> Rebelled against the belly; thus accused it:
> That only like a gulf it did remain
> I' the midst o' the body, idle and unactive,
> Still cupboarding the viand, never bearing
> Like labour with the rest, where the other instruments
> Did see and hear, devise, instruct, walk, feel,
> And, mutually participate, did minister
> Unto the appetite and affection common
> Of the whole body . . .

The belly calms the revolt of the other members by explaining:

> True it is, my incorporate friends, quoth he,
> That I receive the general food at first,
> Which you do live upon; and fit it is;

[53] Titus Livius, *Ab Urbe Condita*, II, 32.

71

> Because I am the store-house and the shop
> Of the whole body: but, if you do remember,
> I send it through the rivers of the blood,
> Even to the court, the heart, to the seat o' the brain;
> And, through the cranks and offices of man,
> The strongest nerves and most inferior veins
> From me receive the natural competency
> Whereby they live.[54]

The origin of the fable is uncertain. But since it was already known to Livy (fl. c. 30 B.C.) there can be no doubt that it is long before the Christian era. When we now read certain passages in St Paul, it is difficult to escape the impression that this story at least suggested to him the very concrete vision of the Church as a fellowship in "one body".

In Rom 12:4–8 we read, "For as in one body we have many members, and all the members do not have the same function, so we, though many, are one body in Christ, and individually members one of another. Having gifts that differ according to the grace given to us, let us use them: if prophecy, in proportion to our faith; if service, in our serving; he who teaches, in his teaching; he who exhorts, in his exhortation; he who contributes, in liberality; he who gives aid, with zeal; he who does acts of mercy, with cheerfulness." Here the fellowship of believers is compared to a body. The emphasis is on our mutual links and consensus. Just as the members together form a body in harmony, so too the various gifts of Christians must not disturb their mutual unity but build it up. It is noticeable that the fellowship of the Church is described here less in terms of a hierarchy than of an organism. The unity is due to the plurality

[54] Act I, scene 1.

of forms and must never be confused with uniformity. The mutual union by which we Christians are linked together as "one body" is "in Christ".

Paul had already pointed to this factor in the sixth chapter of the letter. What he means by "in Christ" is there worked out with reference to baptism. In the passage already cited above from 1 Cor 10:16–17, which was written earlier than Romans, he had already pointed to the unity which results from the Eucharist. The next chapter of that letter goes on to deal with the Eucharistic gatherings in the Church of Corinth. It is well known that this still very unintegrated community had great difficulty in maintaining mutual fellowship. Paul therefore links up directly with his exposition of the Eucharist and goes on in the twelfth chapter to give the following instruction: "For just as the body is one and has many members, and all the members of the body, though many, are one body, so it is with Christ. For by one Spirit we were all baptized into one body — Jews or Greeks, slaves or free — and were all made to drink of one Spirit. For the body does not consist of one member but of many. If the foot should say, 'Because I am not a hand, I do not belong to the body,' that would not make it any less a part of the body. And if the ear should say, 'Because I am not an eye, I do not belong to the body,' that would not make it any less a part of the body. If the whole body were an eye, where would be the hearing? If the whole body were an ear, where would be the sense of smell? But as it is, God arranged the organs in the body, each one of them, as he chose. If all were a single organ, where would the body be? As it is, there are many parts, yet one body. The eye cannot say to the hand, 'I have no need of you,' nor again the head to the feet, 'I have no need of you'.

On the contrary, the parts of the body which seem to be weaker are indispensable, and those parts of the body which we think less honourable we invest with the greater honour, and our unpresentable parts are treated with greater modesty, which our more presentable parts do not require. But God has so adjusted the body, giving the greater honour to the inferior part, that there may be no discord in the body, but that the members may have the same care for one another. If one member suffers, all suffer together; if one member is honoured, all rejoice together. Now you are the body of Christ and individually members of it" (1 Cor 12:12–27).

Clearly, the fable used by Menenius Agrippa had a great success among ancient writers. The early Christian preachers used it to inculcate as vividly as possible the bonds which united the faithful by virtue of the mystery of the Eucharist. Thirty years after the death of Paul the still quarrelsome Corinthians were again called to order by means of the same metaphor. Rome writes to the Church of Corinth: "The greater cannot exist without the lesser and the lesser without the greater. There is a sort of mingling throughout and this is what is advantageous. Take for example the body. The head is nothing without the feet and the feet nothing without the head, but the least members of our body are necessary and useful for the whole body, indeed all works together and is also subordinated to the maintenance of the whole body. So then, let the whole body remain solid in Christ Jesus and let each one be subject to his neighbour, according to the grace given him." [55]

In Paul's own preaching the metaphor of the one body had given rise to further refinements. Having been used primarily

[55] Clement of Rome, *Epistula ad Corinthios*, 37, 4 – 38, 1.

to bring out the need for unity among Christians, it appears in the epistles of the captivity as a means of making still more clear the identification of the fellowship of the Church with Christ. The transition may be outlined as follows. In the great letters just cited (Rom and Cor) Paul propounds to the faithful the truth that they all form one body and hence are in an organic union with each other. In the Letters to the Ephesians and the Colossians he goes a step further by affirming that they are *the* body of Christ and hence are organically united with Christ, the head of the Church.[56] It is symptomatic of this development that while in 1 Cor 12 : 12, as we have seen, the "head" is still regarded as one of the many members of the body, in Eph 4 : 15; 5 : 23 and Col 2 : 19, for instance, Christ is designated as the head and thus has a completely unique position in the body. Now that the fellowship of the Church is thus called the body of Christ, a fundamental reality has been evoked. As believers enter the sphere of Jesus' eucharistic gifts with real faith, from being separate they are moulded into a new reality, they constitute a *communio*, a fellowship. And since this takes place because they identify themselves with Jesus' own expression of obedience to the Father — the sacrifice of the last supper and the cross — the new fellowship can rightly be called the "body of Christ". Here too it is true that no "physical" change can be experimentally verified. But the designation is more than merely a pious metaphor. He who believes and loves has been given a sixth sense, as it were, which

---

[56] See P. Benoit, *Exégèse et Théologie*, II (1961), pp. 107–77; L. Cerfaux, *La théologie de l'Église suivant Saint Paul* (2nd ed., 1965), pp. 223–40; on the origin of the term "body of Christ" in St Paul, see for example R. Schnakkenburg, *The Church in the New Testament* (1965).

enables him to penetrate beyond the superficial realities. What he there finds is no doubt not a scientifically demonstrable reality, but it is undoubtedly a "mystery"-reality in the sense explained above. — If it is to be possible to penetrate beyond the region of sensible experiment and attain this profounder reality there is need of testimony. The new state of things which is reached by faith is not accessible to those who are outside, unless the community which now forms the body of Christ also confesses this faith. If we visit someone who has received a number of presents, we can only know from his own testimony which of the presents has a special significance for him. That one particular gift embodies for him the love of another person cannot be deduced from the gift itself. For this reason the preaching of the Church has a pre-eminent significance. Both to stimulate faith within the community itself and to be an invitation with regard to others, the Church needs to be preached as "event". In one way or another the believers have to make it plain that they are deeply convinced that they form the body of Christ. This sense of duty, which is not a necessity imposed from without but proceeds from the dynamism of the event itself, can also be observed in Jesus himself. His profoundest reality could not be deduced merely from his human appearance. It was only by his preaching by word and deed that it was possible to see in him the embodiment of the salvific will of God. That is why Jesus could say: "If I had not come and spoken to them, they would not have sin" (Jn 15: 22). We are perhaps inclined in such considerations to concentrate too exclusively on the word of preaching. In an age in which the world is filled with the resonance of ecclesiastical words, it is well to remember that preaching by deeds is mostly more efficient. It need not be in the least a sign of scepticism, indeed, it can be a proof of a healthy realism, when the Church is told to do what it preaches to let men see it in action. A competent "service" in the broadest sense of the word is much more convincing, much more credible, than a spate of Sunday-morning words.

3. The Church after Vatican II

The notion of the Church as the redemptive event, in which real fellowship (and hence the conquest of sin) comes about, is also given expression in the constitution *Lumen gentium* of Vatican II. But the text of the constitution must be read very carefully, and to some extent in the light of the history of its genesis if this inspiring vision is to be clearly recognized. In the very first chapter the Holy Spirit is proclaimed as bestowing on the Church "the unity of fellowship and service" (art. 4). The Latin words here are *communio* and *ministratio*, on which the *relator* commented to the Council fathers that they were translations of the biblical terms *koinonia* and *diakonia*. By thus deliberately choosing these pregnant expressions the Council evokes the memory of a time — the first ages of Christianity — when the Church as fellowship was an event as consciously lived as it was reflected upon. In the New Testament itself, but even still more clearly in the Fathers of the Church in the early centuries it is apparent that the significance of the word "body" and *"koinonia"* (*communio*, fellowship) is to a great extent identical.

In 2 Cor 8:4 the two expressions of Vatican II, "fellowship" and "service" are found together in the same passage. In connection with the collection for Jerusalem, Paul praises the good dispositions of the Churches of Macedonia, who begged of him "the grace and the *fellowship* of *service* on behalf of the saints". They asked to be allowed to join in the collection and hence too in the fellowship of helpful service. In view of what will be discussed in our next section, it is also important to note that service here is not used in the official sense of "ministry" but as a synonym for the community itself. In Gal 2:9–60 a profound difference of opinion between Paul and the Church of Jerusalem was smoothed out when James, Peter and John, who were recognized as the "pillars of the Church" gave Paul "the hand of fellowship". Acknowledged in this way by the Apostles, Paul's activity on behalf of the Gentiles thus became a work of the Church fellowship. Paul points out tactfully to Philemon, the owner of the runaway slave Onesimus, that he must let the "fellowship of the faith" be effective in him. He asks him to make this fellowship an actual fact by treating Onesimus as a brother Christian (Philemon 6). Philemon is to show the same respect to Onesimus as he does to Paul, since both have become his partners *(koinonoi)*, members of the same fellowship (v. 17). We have already noted the eucharistic context of the word "fellowship" in Acts 2:42.

In the Fathers of the first centuries the word used as it were incidentally by Vatican II, *communio*, fellowship, had a rich and very concrete content.[57] It is used primarily of the local

[57] See E. Elert, *Abendmahl und Kirchengemeinschaft in der alten Kirche hauptsächlich des Ostens* (1954), E. T.: *Eucharist and Church Fellowship in the First Four Centuries* (1966); L. Hertling, "Communio und Primat", *Una Sancta* 17 (1962), pp. 91–125; see also s. v. "Koinonia" in *Paristic Greek Lexicon*, fascicule 3 (1964), cols. 762–64; J. Lescrauwaet, "Eucharistische eredienst en kerkelijke eenheid", *Bijdragen* 25 (1964), esp. pp. 127–8.

community united around its head, the bishop, by the Eucharist. This fellowship is an organically constituted body. When difficulties arise the fundamental law is invoked whereby each Christian belongs to the community where he joins in the celebration of the Eucharist. This principle is applied so rigorously that when Christians are travelling through "heretical" territories they bring with them the consecrated hosts from their own community.[58] The bond between the various local communities was also called *communio* or fellowship. If there was a threat of division between communities which had hitherto lived in fellowship with each other, the co-celebration of the Eucharist by the heads of the communities in question was the sign that the *communio* was not broken off. Anicetus and Polycarp gave this sign of friendship at the time of the dispute about the date of Easter.[59] By living in *communio* with one community, a Christian was also united in fellowship with the other Churches which were united with it. The bishops kept lists of the local Churches with whom they lived in fellowship and when the members of their flock travelled abroad, gave them letters to show which community the travellers belonged to. The bishop who received them could then examine his own list to see whether he was living in communion with the travellers' community, and if so, the travellers could take part in the celebration of the Eucharist and also enjoy the hospitality of the strange community. Under difficult circumstances, Athanasius appeals to the fact that he was "admitted to the fellowship and love" of the Church of Rome by its synod.[60] He himself affirms expressly that those who are the leaders of a heretical movement

---

[58] Migne, *PG*, 89, col. 756. [59] *Ibid.* 20, col. 508. [60] *Ibid.* 25, col. 309.

"are not to be admitted to the fellowship".[61] Christians who lived in *communio* with such a separated community "must themselves be excluded from our fellowship".[62] When Basil was accused of keeping up fellowship with heretics, he summoned his accusers to prove "from canonical letters" that this was true, or to show that he had actually admitted such heretics to "the fellowship of prayer".[63] This is the concrete background in Christian antiquity for the expression used by Vatican II for the Church. It shows very clearly that the Church was primarily known as a fellowship organically constituted by the Eucharist.

The same truth is also expressly affirmed by the Council by its insertion of the present second chapter into the constitution on the Church. This is the chapter on the "people of God". Here too the Council made a deliberate choice. Before speaking of the hierarchy, in the third chapter, the Council discusses the Church as the fellowship of all. The coordination commission of the Council had to step in to preserve the sequence of the chapters as it now is.[64] In the presentation it was explained that "the people as a whole must be considered in the first instance," since "in the plan of God the people is in the nature of an end, while the hierarchy is a means directed to this end."[65] The consequences which follow from this view with regard to

---

[61] *Ibid.* 25, col. 688.

[62] *Ibid.* 25, cols. 312–311 and 261.

[63] *Ibid.* 32, col. 638.

[64] Y. Congar, "The Church: The People of God", *Concilium* 1, no. 1 (1965), pp. 7–19.

[65] "Ipse populus eiusque salus est in consilio Dei de ordine finis, dum Hierarchia ut medium ad hunc finem ordinatur. Populus imprimis in sua totalitate considerari debet." *Schema Constitutionis de Ecclesia* (1964), pp. 56 f.

authority in the structures of the Church will be examined in the next section. But it may already be pointed out that the question of the democratization of the Church can hardly be very disturbing for those who have made this truth their own. Even in a democracy, of course, there is need of government and authority, but they should clearly be in the service of the end, which is the fellowship of the people of God itself.

Even in the chapter which gave so much trouble, the third chapter of the Constitution on the Church, dealing with the hierarchy, it is apparent on closer inspection that the Church is to be seen above all as a fellowship. Hence a passage was inserted in art. 26, the import of which was not immediately obvious to all the Council fathers. Some opposed the text, on the ground that they found it "too meditative". The text reads as follows: "This Church of Christ is truly present in all legitimate local congregations of the faithful, which are themselves called Churches in the New Testament, in as much as they are joined to their pastors. For in each place they are the new people called by God, in the Holy Spirit and in great numbers (cf. 1 Thess 1 : 5). In these Churches, by the preaching of the Gospel of Christ, the faithful are gathered and the mystery of the Eucharist is celebrated, 'so that the whole fraternity is joined together through the food and blood of the body of the Lord' (Mozarabic prayer, Migne, *Patres Latini*, XCVI, col. 759). In each community of the altar, under the sacred ministry of the bishop, we are shown the symbol of the charity and 'unity of the mystical body, without which there can be no salvation' (St Thomas, *Summa Theologica*, III, q. 73, a. 3). In these communities, though they may often be small and poor or living in the dispersion, Christ is present, by whose power the one, holy, catholic and apostolic Church is united in fellowship. For 'the participation of the body and blood of Christ simply makes us become that which we consume' (Leo the Great, *Sermon* 63, 7; Migne, *PL,* LIV, col. 357)." Behind this passage lies the fundamental notion which we have signalled above, that the Eucharist and the ecclesial 'body of the Lord' are a unity. This is why the presentation of the document to the fathers called attention to the saying of Augustine: "The Church effects the Eucharist and the Eucharist effects the Church."

It is well known that the Council took great pains with this third chapter in order to reach an exact idea of collegiality. In the passage quoted above, which was inserted into the constitution after the treatment of collegiality (arts. 19—23), we find once more the original inspiration out of which the rather more juridical notion of collegiality developed. It will be noticed that the prayer quoted from the Mozarabic liturgy speaks precisely of the "fraternity" which is brought about by the Eucharist. This indicates the local Church, and, no doubt, the local Church as a totality. There is a collegiality, but it is not confined to the holders of office. The college of bishops is a superstructure which is important for the mutual bonds and the unity between the various local communities, but since the college is a living reality it must be a reflection of the basic form of the Church-event itself: the local community. Ratzinger among others has pointed out that the partially juridical restriction of the Christian brotherhood to an official collegiality appears clearly for the first time in Cyprian.[66] Later still, in Basil, a

---

[66] J. Ratzinger, *Die christliche Brüderlichkeit* (1960); id., "The Pastoral Implications of Episcopal Collegiality", *Concilium* 1, no. 1 (1965), pp. 20–33; id., "Fraternité", *Dictionnaire de la Spiritualité* V, cols. 1141–67.

further restriction can be noticed. Now the name of "brother-hood" is confined only to communities of monks. Earlier, all Christian life was inspired by the conviction that all Christians were brothers, without any distinction, and the Church itself was called "fraternitas" or brotherhood. This was an echo of New Testament usage. In 1 Pet 2 : 17 the following exhortation is addressed to Christians: "Honour all men. Love the brother-hood." In order to join this new brotherhood, it may be neces-sary to leave one's safe old ways. But those who leave parents, brothers or sisters for the sake of Christ will receive back brothers and sisters a hundred times over (Mk 10 : 29). In this new situation "you have only one master, but you are all brothers" (Mt 23 : 8). Hence there is no longer any difference between Jew or Greek, free man or slave, but by virtue of baptism all are one in Christ and together children of God (Gal 3 : 27–28). The ethical consequences of this new situation are clear. What is less clear is whether this enthusiastic aware-ness of the ideal of brotherhood leads one to regard only one's fellow-Christians as brothers. The text just quoted from 1 Pet 2 : 17 suggests that believers should have a different attitude to their fellow-believers than to non-Christians. Paul found it very difficult to cease to regard his Jewish fellow-countrymen as no longer "brothers" in the strict sense (Rom 9 : 1–5). We shall take up this question more fully in the next chapter. Here it must suffice to have indicated the ancient Christian back-ground of the conciliar text on the Church as a brotherhood.

As soon as one has realized what it means to affirm that the basic form of the Church is the constitution of true fellowship and brotherliness, a new light is thrown on many expressions used in theology and preaching, some of which seemed to have lost much of their meaning. In this connection, the Council has thrown into strong relief again both the general priesthood of the faithful and the participation of the Church fellowship in the prophetic office of Christ. Certain Council fathers maintained, apropos of art. 10 of the constitution, that the general priesthood of the faithful was only a pious metaphor, but it was emphatically asserted to the contrary that the word priesthood, as applied to the community, could not be taken in an improper sense. Putting the matter still more strongly, the commission dealing with amendments asserted categorically that not only the ministerial but also the general priesthood was "sacramental" in the true sense of the word.[67] Here too the scriptural background is more fertile than one might suspect at first. In the Christian preaching, an interiorization of the notion of liturgical worship took place. Here the New Testament was taking over a venerable element of Jewish spirituality, which is sometimes expressed in the psalms and in the prophets' criticism of the exteriorization which threatened again and again the liturgical worship of the Jews. Practically the whole concrete life of the Christian is described at one time or another in the New Testament in cultic terms. This means that Christians are not called on to offer "something" to God, but their own selves. By entering the true fellowship in one way or another, they throw their whole lives into their task. Hence Paul exhorts the Romans: "Brethren, present your bodies as a living sacrifice, holy and acceptable to God, which is your spiritual worship." What this involves is described by Paul in the next verse, in a phrase so pregnant that it is almost untranslatable, where he

[67] *Schema Constitutionis de Ecclesia* (1964), pp. 42 f.

calls for a "transformation by the renewal of the mind" (cf. Rom 12 : 2). All Christians must cleanse themselves from dead works, in order to come pure to the worship of the living God (Heb 9 : 14). This inward conversion to the other is given in the Eucharist its visible link with the offering of Christ. For the one Christ, consisting of head and members, there is only one sacrifice. Hence later Augustine could say with perfect accuracy: "The whole sacrifice — we ourselves are this."[68]

We have been to some extent accustomed to localize the participation of "the" Church in the prophetic office of Christ exclusively in the hierarchy. It almost seemed as though the magisterium of the Church enjoyed a monopoly which could not be interfered with. But here too Vatican II throws open a wider perspective, on the basis of the conviction that "the" Church primarily comprises the whole fellowship of faith. We read in art. 12 of the constitution: The whole community of the faithful, who have received the anointing from the Holy One (cf. 1 Jn 2 : 20, 27), cannot err in faith, and this special quality is manifested through the supernatural instinct of faith in the whole people when, "from the bishops down to the uttermost extent of the faithful laity" (cf. St Augustine, *De Praedestinatione Sanctorum,* 14, 27; *PL,* XLIV, col. 980), it displays its universal consent on matters of faith and morals.

This is a passage which needs to be carefully translated and minutely studied. It represents an effort to express a truth which did not figure much in the conventional notions of the Church and its magisterium. This may be deduced at once from the fact that there was a certain amount of opposition to the text among

[68] *Confessiones,* X, 6.

the Council fathers. There was a certain fear that the infallibility in faith, here ascribed to the fellowship of the Church as a whole, did not do justice to the magisterium and in particular, to the primacy of the Pope. Some of the ghosts not laid by Vatican I could be seen to hover over Vatican II. One of the opponents stated his position in the following terms: "The intuition of the faithful is undoubtedly of great importance. But this intuition of faith is not (directly) aroused by the Holy Spirit or directly the work of God. But the intuition of faith makes it clear that the doctrine has been handed down uncorrupted through the centuries to the faithful, by the infallible magisterium. The passive infallibility (of the fellowship of the Church) has always been brought about by the active infallibility (of the magisterium)[69] as an effect by its cause."[70] The background of this objection is fairly clear. The speaker considered that the primary and pre-eminent participation of the Church in the prophetic mission of Christ was given through the magisterium. It is only through the magisterium that the fellowship of the Church as a whole can share in this prophetic mission. But the implications of the passage cited from the constitution would seem to be exactly the opposite. It is first the fellowship of the Church as a whole which is the beneficiary of the influence of the Holy Spirit. The magisterium serves to interpret the instinct of faith in the fellowship. To illustrate this point the commission which had to deal with critical amendments appealed to the investigations of other Council fathers which led to the following conclusions: "1) The most important theologians after the Council of Trent ... teach

[69] The words in brackets are explanations added by the author.
[70] *Schema Constitutionis de Ecclesia* (1964), p. 46.

clearly the infallibility of the faithful in their act of faith. 2) Their mode of reasoning and arguing often goes explicitly 'from the faithful to the hierarchy', or from infallibility in believing to infallibility in the teaching of the faith, and no one saw there any danger for the hierarchy. 3) They also see no danger in maintaining that even the Roman Pontiff must take into account the intuition of faith in believers. But it must not be forgotten that the hierarchical rulers, including therefore even the Pope, likewise belong to the faithful."[71]

It is important to note that the somewhat enigmatic expression "intuition of faith" (instinct of faith, consensus fidelium, sensus fidei) is clearly connected with what one might prefer to call "public opinion" in the Church. There are still regions in the Church where such public opinion can hardly manage to make itself heard on account of the pressure of a teaching authority which feels itself threatened. The authorities in question are undoubtedly motivated by the best of intentions and some give the impression of acting from a painful sense of responsibility. It is to be hoped that the perspective of the Church as renewed by Vatican II (a perspective which is in fact ancient and evangelical) will soon bring this state of affairs to an end. The Council itself was aware that what the Council fathers called in rather technical terms the "instinct of faith" coincided to a great extent with public opinion in the Church. This was apparent as soon as the proposal was made that the Council should speak on public opinion in the Church apropos of art. 37 of the constitution. A commission rejected the proposal on the grounds that public opinion had in fact already

[71] *Ibid.*, p. 46.

been dealt with, for which it referred the movers of the motion to art. 12 of the constitution, quoted above.[72] Thus our faith does not rest on private revelations to individuals but is a public affair. No one has brought this out more clearly than Irenaeus, in his refutation of the Gnostics' claims to private revelations. We must draw the consequence that the conviction of the fellowship of the Church with regard to its faith must be treated with supreme reverence. Here the fellowship enunciates its faith in what is most profoundly its own essence. Changes, shifts and renovations in this consciousness must be given their chance to confront each other in public, and at the present day, of course, must also make use of the modern communications media. If then after some time a somewhat modified "public opinion" crystallizes in the Church, this is a proof that the Church is capable of a new self-understanding in a new age. Christ lives on in the human fellowship of believers which is the Church. This is not a timeless entity but the bearer of salvation and redemption to a world of men which is constantly changing and displaying its need and desire for redemption in constantly changing ways.

4. Authority in the fellowship of the Church

The strong emphasis on the priority of the Church as a fellowship makes it urgent for us, who have to accustom ourselves to this idea, to enquire into the nature and function of authority in the Church. For many, the notions of fellowship and

[72] *Ibid.*, p. 134.

authority seem to be in conflict with each other. All pleas for more "democratization" of the people of God are branded as a threat to the hierarchical structure of the Church. And conversely, there is a reaction at the present day which makes some people feel that every exercise of authority in the Church is detrimental to the fellowship and an infringement on the responsibility of all. Though the concrete problems in this field will hardly be settled for some time, since an outdated ecclesiology cannot be got rid of in a day, a theology both renewed and responsible is already taking shape. This can be outlined without much difficulty in terms of the view of the Church given above. The important thing is that "the" Church is not the ecclesiastical authority, but the fellowship which this authority serves. That the task of the ecclesiastical authorities is to serve is clearly affirmed by Paul. At the very moment when he finds himself compelled to defend his apostolate, he ends his explanation by saying, "We are your servants (or slaves) for Jesus' sake" (2 Cor 4:5). This is the way in which Paul presents himself again and again to the various Churches (Rom 1:1; Phil 1:1). He thus shows that he is profoundly penetrated by Jesus' own example and precepts. "If I then, your Lord and Teacher, have washed your feet, you also ought to wash one another's feet" (Jn 13:14–15).[73] The old despotic form of civil authority is not to be the model for the exercise of power in the Church. "You know that those who are supposed to rule over the Gentiles lord it over them, and their

[73] See Y. Congar, "La hiérarchie comme service selon le Nouveau Testament et les documents de la Tradition", in *L'Épiscopat et l'Église universelle* (1962), pp. 67–99; K. H. Schelkle, *Jüngerschaft und Apostelamt* (1957), E. T.: *Discipleship and Priesthood* (1967).

great men exercise authority over them. But it shall not be so among you; but whoever would be great among you must be your servant, and whoever would be first among you must be slave of all" (Mk 10:42-44; cf. Mt 18:4). This saying, which was uttered in a historical context of the past, does not exclude the possibility of the exercise of authority in modern democracy being taken as a model to some extent for authority in the Church. When one looks back on history, it is difficult to avoid the impression that the Church has copied historical forms of civil authority, but without being flexible enough in the long run to introduce into its own fellowship the process of democratization which took place in the State. Once this fact is recognized, it suggests that there should be a change of attitude both in the official authorities and the mass of the faithful in the Church. It is not perhaps unwarranted at the present time to think of an attitude fundamentally different to that to which we are accustomed. This means that every Christian in every state of life must be convinced and may rightly be convinced that he himself is responsible — or that the community must prove itself, and not the wielders of authority in the first instance. The authorities are in the service of the community. Their function is to help things forward, so that the Church may attain its goal — that of being a redemptive fellowship. Hence it is important to know that in several places in the draft constitutions Vatican II substituted the word "task", "office" (*munus*) where the text had "power" (*potestas*). This links up directly with the passage from art. 4 of the constitution on the Church, which has been quoted above, where the Church was described as being made up of "fellowship and service", *ministratio*, cf. *diakonia*). We may also recall that the explanation of chapter 2 of the constitution contains the words: "The people itself and the salvation of the people belong to the order of ends in God's purpose. The hierarchy is ordained to that end, as a means. The people must first be envisaged as a whole." It follows from all this that all "power" in the Church comes to rest with the authorities through the medium of the fellowship. Their authority is always derived from the end in view. But the fellowship itself is precisely the end in view.

This does not in the least exclude the fact that the authorities in the Church also receive their authority from Christ. Christ willed that the community of believers dedicated to him should be an organized or "structured" community. This is the intention of the long exposition of Paul in 1 Cor 12:4–31. All that serves to build up the fellowship (such gifts as healing, helping, administrating, v. 28) was willed by Christ for the good of the one body. To put this in more abstract terms: by willing the end, Christ also naturally willed the means. It is obvious that the first "wielders of authority" were directly called by Christ himself. The text of Mk 3:13–19 lays some stress upon this point. "He called to him those whom he desired; and they came to him. And he appointed twelve, to be with him, and to be sent out to preach ... And he appointed the twelve." Then the twelve are named one by one. The literal translation, "He made them a twelve," indicates the creation of a function.[74] They served later to preach what they had seen and heard, and thus to assemble round themselves the first fellowship of the Church, which they represented as the twelve.

In these early days the bearers of authority could also ap-

---

[74] See *Receuil Lucien Cerfaux* I (1954), pp. 425–69; W. Burgers, *De instelling van de twaalf in het evangelie van Marcus* (1960).

point their own sucessors, so that for the most part authorities
and fellowship formed a clear and palpable unity. The leaders
were in fact as well as in name representatives of the community, which regarded the acts of the leaders as also pro-
ceeding from the community. The Apostles and their successors clearly functioned organically *within* the community. Their
authority had not yet been transferred, as it were, to people
apart from the fellowship. But as a gap developed between
authority and community and the "psychological" distance
between them became more marked, a greater need was felt
of bringing in the people once more for the appointment of
new bearers of authority. In this way the leader was still
clearly "one of us". It is certain that at the beginning of the
third century the bishops (even in Rome) were chosen by the
people and clergy of the vacant see.[75]

If it is really true, and if it is so experienced by the community, that the wielder of ecclesiastical office is not en-
throned at a distance above the community, but functions
within it, it will be all the easier for such an office-holder to
exercise his authority. In his function of serving the end of the
fellowship, he furthers by his service the very same purpose
as animates the community. As the impulse to resist an authority
aloof from the fellowship grows less when authority is once
more in solidarity with the fellowship, many rationalizations
of feelings hostile to authority will also quickly disappear.
Deep down, men are not "against the government," but against
a detached authority which imagines itself in competition with
the sense of responsibility of an adult fellowship. When

[75] See E. C. Ratcliff, "'Apostolic Tradition': Questions concerning the Appointment of the Bishop", *Studia Patristica* VII (1966), pp. 266–70.

authority is clearly at the service of all — which can only be when it does not in fact place itself outside the fellowship — it can exercise its authority without too much difficulty, because the community recognizes itself in what has been spelled out by the authorities. Obviously, this state of affairs can only be attained by an effective decentralization in the Church. This is in keeping with what has been said above, with some emphasis, about the local eucharistic community being the model and basic form of the Church-event. But it was also made clear that the early Church, which was deeply penetrated by this conviction, never lost sight of the bonds between the local communities. This does in fact create some difficulties in the actual exercise of authority. The life of a local community can only be interpreted with difficulty by a wielder of authority who lives elsewhere. And the rulings of a distant authority can only be recognized with difficulty by the local community as the interpreter of its life. But here too, if we sincerely consider the true nature of the Church, certain lines may be indicated along which future development must probably take place.

First and foremost, an effective decentralization of the Church must be seriously envisaged.[76] The result might be that the central authority would only intervene directly in a local community in extreme cases, and then only when the local authorities are obviously at fault. It is a manifestation of true *communio*, and hence of the very nature of the Church, if the

---

[76] See the Decree on Ecumenism, art. 4: "While preserving unity in essentials, let all members of the Church, according to the office entrusted to each, preserve a proper freedom in the various forms of spiritual life and discipline, in the variety of liturgical rites, and even in the theological elaborations of revealed truth."

local authorities have the full confidence of the supreme authority. Secondly, the local authorities must govern in real mutual collegiality. This obliges them to remain in constant contact with their colleagues and hence with the central authority. The Church of the West might well be guided by the principle formulated by Vatican II for the Eastern Churches: The Ordinaries of the various individual Churches which have jurisdiction in the same territory should, by taking common counsel in regular meetings, strive to promote unity of action (*Orientalium Ecclesiarum*, art. 4).

Finally, and this is the most delicate point, it must be the task of the local ordinaries to implement in their particular Churches what they have recognized as the authentic means of promoting fellowship, in the course of their collegial contacts.[77] Decentralization of the fellowship of the Church is not national or local sectarianism. Such "parochialism" has often been a threat to the Church and can be so again. It is well to remember the ironical comment of Augustine on the local sectarianism of the Donatists: "Do they think that the whole world has gone bad, while only Africa is sweet?"[78] The Bishop of Hippo solemnly opted out of this African particularism. Only a continuous and well-balanced exchange between the local community and the universal Church can preserve Christians from this sort of pernicious sectarianism. Just at the moment when Christians are becoming more fully conscious of the relevance of the local Church, it is more necessary than ever to use great

---

[77] See F. W. Kantzenbach, "Communio Sanctorum, Kirche und Konzil", *Oecumenica. Jahrbuch für ökumenische Forschung* (1966), pp. 149–78; esp. 168–77.
[78] Migne, *PL*, XXXVI, col. 371.

perspicacity and prudence. Otherwise, instead of re-discovering the promised lands, so to speak, they will find themselves stranded on desert islands. Prudence is particularly called for when the notion that the tension between the universal and the local Churches is due to external historical forces penetrates wider circles. But when the historical conditions which led to the development of a centralizing ecclesiology in the West are recognized, it should be easier to restore their due honour to the Eastern traditions of the Church as a fellowship of local Churches.[79]

Difficulties with regard to the exercise of authority are felt most acutely in limit situations. This has always been the case. The exercise of the "magisterium" or teaching authority of the Church needs to be given special consideration here. As we have seen, authority only exists in order to serve the fellowship of the Church in its effort to attain its common goal. This goal may be described as the actual self-dedication to Christ in faith, which is verified in a very concrete and concentrated form during great sacramental celebrations. Here dedication to Christ is embodied in the concrete in dedication to one another. The fellowship which is brought about in the sacraments — if it is genuine — will inspire and illuminate the whole of daily life. Thus one places one's faith and confidence in another, who is Christ. The self-dedication of faith has thereby gained concrete content. This specific meaning is transmitted to us by the preaching of the Church, especially at the celebration of the Eucharist (cf. Rom 10:17). The magisterium

[79] See Y. Congar, "De la communion des églises à une ecclésiologie de l'Église universelle", in *L'Épiscopat et l'Église universelle* (1962), pp. 227-60.

can and must insist if needs be in certain cases on the content of the Christian message, where, for instance, the specific goal of (Christian) fellowship might otherwise be endangered. The Church believes — and therefore can never "prove" — that a genuine *communio*, a redemptive fellowship, is possible, especially in the name of Christ (Acts 4 : 12). Those who strive to bring it about otherwise, not in explicit confession of faith in Christ, should not be resisted by the Church. On the contrary, we must realize that fellowship, even solid fellowship, is quite possible without explicit confession of faith in Christ. But the Church offers the possibility of bringing it about precisely in the common profession of faith, in word and deed, in the name of Christ. Those who specifically reject this offer can obviously be notified that they no longer belong to this fellowship in the strict sense. This was done in the early Church. If someone preached "another gospel," the *communio* or fellowship was considered to have been broken off. Excommunication followed — the express termination of the bond with the fellowship which had in fact already been renounced. It has been noted in this connection that in Christian antiquity there was no exact definition of those who had the right to pronounce an excommunication.[80] In fact, dissidents excommunicated themselves. Hence here too all that the bearers of authority eventually did was "interpret" a situation already existing within the community itself. Cyprian has preserved a letter of Firmilian addressed to Pope Stephen during the controversy about re-baptism. Here the upholder of the position, eventually declared heretical, put the matter as follows: "You yourself

[80] See L. Hertling, "Communio und Primat", *Una Sancta* 17 (1962), p. 106.

have committed the great sin by cutting yourself off from so many communities. You have excommunicated yourself. Remember: a schismatic is one who puts himself outside the *communio* of the Church."[81]

But these are only the difficult limit-situations in which ecclesiastical authority has to be exercised. There is also a very ordinary way in which the magisterium functions. This distinction is important at a time when many find it difficult to recognize the nature of the priestly office. Too much emphasis has been laid on the purely sacramental and liturgical aspect of the task of the pastor. His function as apostolic preacher was almost totally lost to sight. If it is thrown into stronger relief, it will be possible to see better how this office also participates in the service given by the magisterium. A good deal of priestly work may be devoted to interpreting what goes on in the hearts of the faithful. If we try to determine in the concrete all the factors which are useful and necessary to such interpretation, we find ourselves in front of a broad programme, at the very moment when there is uncertainty about the faith. To interpret means first of all to listen intently for a long time. This can be done in many ways, as for instance by letting those who put their complaints to the priests really speak out their hearts. This is in itself a duty of pastoral care. If the priest then succeeds in being a proper sounding-board — "playback" — so that the layman feels that he has been understood, a type of redemption is often accomplished at once in a modest way. There is communication and solidarity. The work of the priest consists to no small extent in offering the redemptive word. This is the word in which the other recognizes himself

[81] Migne, *PL*, III, col. 1174.

and knows at the same time that it now also comes to him from others. The whole process of active hearing, and then translating and interpreting with all due reserve, demands along with a truly pastoral prudence a certain technical command of dialogue and of theology.

A similar process must also be envisaged to a certain extent on the higher level of official Church preaching, which must be in its own way a reflection and an interpretation of the infallible faith of the Church fellowship.[82] This interpretation and re-statement of the instinct of faith as it works in the faithful must on occasion be dogmatic in nature, as we saw above when considering some limit-situations. A truth is enunciated and hence is established as validly formulated for a given age and in a given situation. This need not imply a questionable fluidity, provided that one does not consider dogma in a way which is too abstract and universal and too little in the sense of a local confession. The dogmatic formulas of the first Councils of the Church have been and still are the prayer of the Church in the liturgy, where they are included in the confession of faith. Dogmatic statements are the embodiment and interpretation of the instinct of faith in the community and not an extrinsic, juridical entity in which the fellowship of the Church has no part.

The government of the Church will of course also be regulated by the end and object of the Church. This "power" exists

---

[82] See the Christmas Pastoral of the Netherlands Episcopate, 1960 (*Herderlijk Schrijven van Nederlands Episcopaat van Kerstmis,* 1960 [1961]); see also J. C. Groot, on the "Horizontal Aspects" of collegiality, in G. Baraúna, ed., *De Ecclesia. Beiträge zur Konstitution "Über die Kirche",* II (1966), p. 90, where he points out that the "communio fidelium" forms a norm for the "communio episcoporum", which being essentially a special form of the "communio fidelium" must function according to the "consensus fidelium" which is prior to the "consensus episcoporum".

in the Church, in order that the fellowship may be realized in an efficient manner in the necessary organized structures. There is of course the danger that genuine fellowship may be impeded by its own organization, which may lose sight of its character as service and make itself an end in itself. This would be a sort of perversion, a reversal of the true order of things. But the recognition of the possibility of such dangers should not lead to an exaggerated action in the other direction. Every Church fellowship demands a minimum of "Church order" and discipline. A description of the demands with which such a Church order should comply would mean repeating much of what has already been said. Such a Church order should be de-centralized to allow of local government to the greatest possible extent and hence the greatest possible pluralism. If it is constituted in this way it can also be revised more easily in view of changing circumstances, without having to have recourse to time-consuming procedures. The framers of such constitutions must also be prepared to impose a great deal of moderation on themselves, above all by restricting themselves to the main outlines.

The guiding principle throughout must be the profound conviction that the Church must be above all a genuine fellowship and thus the place of redemption. Such a fellowship can only come about when every member of the people of God recognizes his own indispensable responsibility and is able to exercise it. As long as authority, whether it be that of God himself or of an ecclesiastical superior, is seen as in competition with human responsibility, it is as good as dead. If authority succeeds in establishing itself clearly and organically as service within the fellowship, there will be very little place for any sense of dissatisfaction in the Church.

IV

WORLD-WIDE REDEMPTION

1. Historical changes

A French writer of 1831 put the following speech on the lips of a philosopher who was addressing a Christian: "I know that there was once a Cardinal who finished reading the *Phaedo* with the sigh: 'Holy Socrates, pray for me.' But that made a heretic of the Cardinal for the moment . . . The absolute damnation of the vast majority of mankind is the necessary consequence of your system."[83] Centuries earlier, Bernard of Clairvaux had at any rate to some extent justified the philosopher's opinion. That was the time when he found to his dismay that Plato had been regarded as a Christian by Abelard. The "honey-tongued doctor" remarked very critically that Abelard thus proved himself to be a heretic.[84] This sally of Bernard must undoubtedly have been strongly conditioned by the actual historical circumstances. If he were alive today, he would be reading many publications about "anonymous Chris-

---

[83] P. Leroux, *Encyclopédie nouvelle* III (1831), p. 558; cf. L. Capéran, *Le problème du salut des infidèles. Essai historique* (2nd ed., 1934), p. 470.
[84] Migne, *PL*, CLXXXII, col. 1062.

tians," the value of "implicit faith" or salvation without the Gospel. His holy indignation might well be kindled as regards an ecumenical council which could make a declaration on non-Christian religions which was definitely positive.

But this is an unreal hypothesis. Bernard cannot come back, because history does not repeat itself. Our present situation, which also conditions to some extent the self-understanding of the Church, is very different from that of the abbot of Clairvaux. But if we did in fact look for historical parallels, it would seem that in one point at least our present situation displays a more marked agreement with the early Church than with the Middle Ages. The first Christians knew well that they were only a small group in a world-wide empire. This notion disappeared quickly enough, because Christianity spread rapidly and the regions to which the Gospel had not been preached remained totally outside the perspective of Christians. It was possible, as a result, in the early Middle Ages, to imagine that the Church spanned practically the whole inhabited world. Now that the voyages of discovery have long since opened up new worlds, which have been brought home to us in our own days by the modern communications media, we are once more returning — with some difficulty — to accept the notion that Christianity is geographically and chronologically a small affair and of recent origin.

This new realization, though it is not the only factor at work, has helped to make the problem of the relationship between the Church and the world an urgent one once more. How does the Church understand itself in relation to time and space? In view of the preceding chapters, it might well be asked whether all this inward-looking analysis of the Church has much realism about it. Once one is convinced of the fact that even at the present day, and almost certainly in the future, the Church can embrace only a tiny group of men, which vanishes almost to nothingness in comparison with those who have never heard of Christianity or refuse to consider it — must not Christian theology have an air of unreality about it? For many centuries the cry could be heard in the Church: "Outside the Church there is no salvation." If we remind ourselves that Church history coincides only with a small fraction of world history, such an expression of self-assurance may well seem to be a grotesque exaggeration of our own importance.

In the beginning, Christians did not over-estimate themselves in this way. Paul undoubtedly recognizes a distinction between those outside and those within, but adds in the same breath: "What have I to do with judging outsiders?" (1 Cor 5:12). He had already urged his brothers in the faith not to give any offence to outsiders (1 Thess 4:12). The general trend of this remark leaves little room for excommunication and reprobation of those who refuse to belong to the Church. The apostolic exhortation points in a totally different direction. There is a distinction between the Church and the world, between the fraternity and the rest, but there can be no question of prejudiced hostility. "Honour all men. Love the brotherhood" (1 Pet 2:17) is an exhortation which is practically identical with Paul's, "Do good to all men, especially to those who are of the household of the faith" (Gal 6:10). It may even be seen that the synoptic gospels display a clearly marked tendency to break with the Jewish tradition which included only fellow-countrymen among the "neighbour" (cf. Mt 5:43–48). When the question, "Who is my neighbour?" is explicitly asked, the

answer in Luke is absolutely clear. It is not primarily the fel-
low-Israelite, not the priest or levite, but the Samaritan who
was moved to compassion.[85] The sense of mission with which
the first Christians were inspired was no obstacle. It rather
moved them to intense effort. They were profoundly convinced
that they could offer something to the "others": faith in the
redeemer Jesus Christ. Such a conviction can easily tend to
become a sense of superiority. Possibly Paul was already warning the faithful against this when he wrote to his fellow-
Christians at Colossae: "Conduct yourselves wisely towards
outsiders, making the most of the time. Let your speech always
be gracious, seasoned with salt, so that you may know how you
ought to answer every one" (Col 4:5-6).

As those outside the Church took up a more hostile attitude,
the inner solidarity of the fellowship of believers grew stronger.
This is a well-known phenomenon, a sociological law. In time
of war internal dissensions disappear, to make way for a keen
sense of comradeship. But such extrinsic factors can obscure the
positive reasons which bind the fellowship together, its over-
riding final common end. Men come together to form a common
front against the attacker, and the task of self-defence distracts
them from their positive tasks. At the time of the great persecu-
tions under the Roman empire, something of the kind can be
noted in North Africa. The inward look of the Church fellowship is reinforced by the appearance of dissident groups. An
"introvert" ecclesiology took shape of which Bishop Cyprian
was a typical representative. The lapidary formula, "Extra

---

[85] See J. Ratzinger, *Die christliche Brüderlichkeit* (1960); J. B. Souček, "Der
Bruder und der Nächste", in *Hören und Handeln, Festschrift Ernst Wolf*
(1962), pp. 362–71.

ecclesiam nulla salus," is taken from his writings. "Outside the Church there is no salvation" was to become the slogan of an embattled and belligerent Christianity.

It is of more than historical interest to note that this expression formed part of a process of reasoning, the conclusion of which was explicitly rejected by an important part of the Church. The conflict was concerned with the validity of baptism administered by dissident groups. Tertullian and Cyprian, along with many of the Churches of the East, maintained strongly that such baptism was futile.[86] If one of these separated brethren later joined the Church, he had to be baptized again. The general principle on which Cyprian bases himself to reach this practical conclusion is that there is nowhere at all outside the Church where salvation can be attained. "Hence" even a baptism administered outside the Church cannot bestow salvation. There was so much disagreement about this conclusion in the Church of the West that it was only perhaps the martyrdom of the two great opponents, Cyprian and Pope Stephen, which prevented a schism. But the Church of Rome did not waver in its conviction that baptism conferred in the name of the Father, Son and Holy Spirit, even if given within a heretical group, was undoubtedly an authentically Christian reality. The Council of Arles in 314, at which Africans were also present, confirmed this doctrine. One remarkable consequence of the whole episode, however, is that in spite of the rejection of the conclusion drawn by the Africans, the principle on which they had built up their theory came in the end to find a welcome in the Church of

[86] See P. van Leeuwen, "Grenzen van Kerk en doop", *Jaarboek Werkgenootschap katholische theologen in Nederland* 1965–66 (1966), pp. 71–102; F. Kantzenbach, *op. cit.*, note 77 above.

Rome. The Church of the West also went on to make more and more use of the dubious axiom, "Outside the Church there is no salvation".

It is very probable that the clear-sighted circumspection of Augustine had much to do with this phenomenon, contrary to his own intention. Then as now, fine shades of meaning are apt to be missed. It is easier to popularize clear-cut slogans than subtle distinctions. Augustine had great respect for Cyprian, whom he revered as a saint.[87] Nonetheless, he did not share all his opinions. Augustine could not of course say this bluntly. He preferred to make use of more prudent formulations. "'There is no salvation outside the Church', says Cyprian. Who would want to deny this? Hence it is true that all that one receives from the Church does not count for salvation outside the Church. But it is one thing not to have something, and another to have it fruitlessly."[88] Augustine could hardly have expressed more gently his opposition to Cyprian. A few pages later he allows himself to speak even more clearly. "Some of those who are baptized outside the Church, are really counted by God's foreknowledge among those who are baptized within the Church, because the water of baptism begins to work their salvation even there (outside the Church)."[89] But Augustine's careful nuances with regard to Cyprian escaped his less sensitive successors. A century later Fulgentius of Ruspe thought he was rendering the mind of Augustine exactly when he declared roundly: "It is absolutely certain that not only all pagans but also all Jews and heretics and schismatics who die

[87] Migne, *PL*, XLIII, cols. 223–5.
[88] *Ibid.*, col. 170.
[89] *Ibid.*, cols. 196–7, which is not taken sufficiently into account by H. B. Weijland in his *Augustinus en de kerklijke tucht* (1965), pp. 178–94.

outside the Church will go into the eternal fire which is prepared for the devil and his angels." [90] The damage is already
done. The carefully formulated doctrine of Augustine is put in
the shop-window along with cuttings of historical interest, all
under the label chosen by a hasty compiler. The misunder-
standing became definitive when the work of Fulgentius in
which the crude statement appeared was attributed to Augustine
by later copyists. Thus the principle, "Outside the Church there
is no salvation" gained an authority in the Middle Ages which
was almost unquestionable. Alcuin, Ratramnus, Ivo of Chartres,
Abelard, Peter Lombard and Thomas Aquinas were not better
informed about the supposed authorship of Augustine. [91]

When then the Church was forced by the voyages of discovery in the fifteenth and sixteenth centuries to recognize its
geographical limitations, Christian realism also sought more
room for manoeuvre. The margin offered by the falsely canonized tradition was not great. But theologians sought to save
themselves by means of various distinctions, designed to break
through the narrow limits of the assertion, "Outside the Church
there is no salvation". Throughout all these efforts, there was an
underlying sense of realities which was of great importance.

Christians were profoundly penetrated by their faith in
God's redemptive love and mercy, and recognized the ab-
surdity of the assumption that the vast majority of mankind
were not to share in salvation. Hans Urs von Balthasar has
described this attitude very vividly. "The medieval castle where
there could be dancing and feasting high above the torture-

---

[90] Migne, *PL*, XL, col. 776; LXV, col. 704.
[91] See J. Beumer, "Zwischen Patristik und Scholastik", *Gregorianum* 23
(1942), pp. 326–47.

chambers and dungeons have collapsed and will never be re-built. No Christian will now dance while his brothers are being tortured." [92] But a habit of thought which has been settled for centuries can become a trauma. There was proof of this during the Second Vatican Council. The Council fathers had shown in the Dogmatic Constitution on the Church, and the Pastoral Constitution on the Church in the Modern World, that they had undoubtedly come to discover that the Church has no monopoly of salvation. Nonetheless, they were still under the spell of their own and our past. On the occasion of arts. 15 and 16 of the Constitution on the Church, a text was drafted which envisaged both non-Roman Catholic Christians and the various groups of non-Christians in a very positive way. Mis-givings were voiced. There was some fear that "the positive tendency (of this passage) could fortify non-Catholics in their negative attitude; and likewise that Catholics who find Catho-lic morals a grave burden might waver in their belief". [93] Behind these well-intentioned remarks there is a questionable sense of superiority which has not yet been completely eliminated. Even at present there are anonymous writers who display an un-mistakable feeling of resentment because the Church refuses to ascribe to itself a total monopoly with regard to redemption and salvation. [94] But the Church has ceased to do so, because our eyes have been re-opened to the signs of the times. When Vatican II, in art. 16 of the Constitution on the Church, ascribes in succession to Jews, Muslims, the followers of non-Christian

[92] See H. Urs von Balthasar, *Schleifung der Bastionen* (1952), p. 53.
[93] "Ne tenor nimis positivus acatholicos in suo acatholicismo firmet, catho-licis vero, quibus moralitas catholica onerosa est, infirmet", *Schema Con-stitutionis de Ecclesia* (1964), p. 50.
[94] Gregorius Rhenanus, *Aufbruch oder Zusammenbruch* (1966), p. 6.

religions and finally to men without any religion who strive for true justice and peace the possibility of receiving God's salvation, the Church has in practice come to hold an opinion diametrically opposed to that of Fulgentius of Ruspe. His catalogue of doom, which dominated tradition so long, has now been taken up again but with the co-efficients changed. In the Pastoral Constitution on the Church in the Modern World the Council declares: "For, since Christ died for all men (Rom 8:32), and since the ultimate vocation of man is in fact one, and divine, we ought to believe that the Holy Spirit in a manner known only to God offers to every man the possibility of being associated with this paschal mystery" (art. 22).

The immediate question which arises in view of all this is both simple and menacing: why does the Church still exist? Directly after the positive paragraphs dealing with non-Catholics Vatican II placed a paragraph dealing with the missionary task of the Church. The very fact that the transition from the one theme to the other is left unexplained is a sign of an unanswered difficulty. Once the question is said to be "menacing," it seems that one is thereby affirming one's intention to hold fast to the special place of the Church in the world. As far as we are concerned, this is indeed the case. It seems to me wrong to trouble the "others" with our effort to make the just rights of the Church acceptable at the present day. But those who believe in the Church's right to exist must undoubtedly give an account *to themselves* of the fundamental truth of their faith. This can still be of interest to the others for two reasons. Firstly, because they are trying along with the fellowship of the Church to make the world which all inhabit a place fit to live in. Then, from the standpoint of solidarity, they can also be interested in the way in which the Church understands itself precisely when in confrontation with them. Consequently, those whom Paul called "outsiders" will wish to see to it that the self-legitimation of the Church is not established at their expense. In other words, they will at once take up a critical and defensive attitude as soon as the self-justification of the Church violates in any way the general solidarity of mankind.

2. Salvation outside the Church

The question which we have now reached seems to have been given an unambiguous answer in the testimony of Peter before the Jewish authorities. Speaking of "Jesus Christ of Nazareth, whom you crucified", he says, "There is salvation in no one else, for there is no other name under heaven given among men by which we must be saved" (Acts 4:12). If this saying is taken as an objective communication and not as a confession of faith, sentence has been passed. The consequence must be exclusivism and apartheid. Fanatical zeal, crusades and even inquisitions could then be justified by this text. This was clearly understood by Lessing when he wrote of the Christian Daia that she had to inflict torment out of love — and could not do otherwise, since to permit a friend to stray from the truth of Christianity was to let that friend fall into eternal perdition.[95]

The meaning to be given to Acts 4:12 can only be made clear when we allow ourselves to take a new perspective on the basis of the New Testament itself. In Mt 25:31 ff. there is a picture of the last judgment. The Son of man divides man-

[95] *Nathan the Wise*, V, 6.

kind into two groups beside him, one on the left and one
on the right. He says to those on his right: "Come, o
blessed of my Father, inherit the kingdom prepared for you
from the foundation of the world; for I was hungry and you
gave me food, I was thirsty and you gave me drink, I was a
stranger and you welcomed me, I was naked and you clothed
me, I was sick and you visited me, I was in prison and you
came to me." So far there is little to astonish us in this picture.
These men's faith had obviously been exercised in works of
mercy. But the astonishing thing is that these men seem never
to have recognized their Lord. They go on to ask: "Lord, when
did we see thee hungry and feed thee, or thirsty and give thee
drink? And when did we see thee a stranger and welcome thee,
or naked and clothe thee? And when did we see thee sick or
in prison and visit thee?" The denouement of the scene comes
with the answer of the Lord: "As you did it to one of the least
of these my brethren, you did it to me." Clearly, one can
encounter the Lord without knowing it. Those who really give
themselves to their fellow-men give by this very fact testimony
to their "faith". They show by their acts that they are ready
to pay reverence to the mystery of other men. By being kind
and helpful, men cease to try to manipulate others as a sort of
extension of themselves. The Christian recognizes in such goodness the presence of God's creative grace. But he should not
feel it necessary that the others *must* also interpret it in this
way. Hence the expression "anonymous Christians" can be
misleading. The goodness which Christians discover in the
world is *for them* the presence of Christian grace and Christian
redemption. But they are then interpreting it in the light of their
faith. Those who do not hold this explicit faith can of course

reject such an explanation, especially if they feel that they are thus being annexed by the Christian system. But it is then well to see exactly how matters stand. It will be seen that practically everyone has such experiences in his life, without finding them unbearable. Whether I know it or not, my existence can be given an interpretation in another's world of meaning which escapes me. Only when the expression "anonymous Christianity" is not taken as an interpretation within the world of Christian meaning, but as an objective, universally valid description of facts can there be really misunderstandings. This always happens when two types of language are confused.

Examples are ready to hand and they give us to understand that we are dealing here with a much more widespread phenomenon. In his second *Duineser Elegie* the poet Rilke says to his beloved: "You penetrate into my blood. This room, this springtime feels itself with you." This is not a biochemically verifiable statement. Those who take it as such will be ready to prove conclusively, by means of their scientific instruments if necessary, that the lenten blossoms do not change when they become the setting for a love-scene. This is perhaps even clearer in the passage where Ina Seidel describes the transformation which takes place in the world when the heart is filled with love. "The hand, the face of every man, the obscure look of every beast, every tree which bends before the wind, every cornfield, every stalk of grass along the way, every handful of earth and the sun with all the stars; the whole created world seemed to her his mirror, and as though she only needed to know the right formula to make him appear."[96] The face of every man seemed to her to be his reflection. In the same way,

[96] Ina Seidel, *Das Wunschkind* (1964), p. 277.

Christians may call all forms of genuine human fellowship "anonymous Christianity". It is an interpretation in the light of the Christian faith, just as in the example quoted the face of every man is read in the light of a personal love. For those who are not themselves involved in this relationship such words cannot be offensive. They take into account the special usage which is made here of language. It is not scientific language but the language of faith. The varieties of language mirror the various facets of a complex reality which is made up of many fields of meaning. Both those who hold that the world of their faith is the only reality, and those who hold that the world of science is the only reality are making a mistake. Reality has several dimensions.

Hence the term "anonymous Christianity" gives us to understand that Christians believe in the reality of redemption outside the Church. There is no sense in trying to localize it exactly, and indeed it cannot be done. But it will be well to offer some general considerations here to avoid undue restrictions.

In very different cultures and throughout all religions the relationship of man and woman in marriage and family signifies one of the most concrete possibilities of fellowship and hence of redemption. Hence it is not surprising that this "universally human" relationship is expressly drawn into the event of redemption by sacred Scripture. What Paul writes in Eph 5 is a clear example of a Christian interpretation of a universal human fact. Hence husband and wife who surrender themselves to each other's freedom and, above all, who undertake to let each other's freedom grow through daily life, are able to redeem each other. Certainly in our own culture this is one of the most concrete possibilities of bringing about redemption from the selfishness of sin. Paul throws light on this human reality by means of his faith in the redemption through Christ: husband and wife are the way in which the redeeming Christ appears to each of them. Here we have the Christian interpretation of a very concrete element of life, which is undoubtedly constantly changing, but often shows nonetheless a number of similar structures. In the changing circumstances of life, which are not contained by the bounds of any Church, the mutual redemption of husband and wife is itself an event which can never be sealed into one moment of grace. Every married person can here think of his own experiences. There are many examples in literature: the tranquil "natural growth" of fidelity in Philemon and Baucis, [97] the marriage of Ulysses and Penelope, sorely tried by adventures and accidents. In the dramatic proportions of Othello's jealousy, on which his marriage to Desdemona founders, in the young love of Romeo and Juliet, in Madame Bovary's loathing of what she sees as the bourgeois inanity of her husband, every man recognizes something of himself, of his possibilities and impotence, of all the challenges to which the married life of everyone is exposed. In and through the many tasks which married life imposes on husband and wife, fellowship and redemption can come about. At the same time, this possibility, which is not confined to any religion, opens up a further perspective. The happy fellowship of two persons can fall victim to a new exclusiveness. But then one egoism takes the place of another. True fellowship admits of spheres of greater or less intimacy but excludes nobody. Hence married love contains at least radically the possibility

[91] See H. Haasse, "Liefde en geluk", *Het Huwelijk* (1965), pp. 156 ff.

of parental love. Mutual fellowship is seen to be ready on principle to admit new human life into its own realm.

With this, the question is also raised about all concrete possibilities of fellowship on the widest of scales. Christians have very often been inclined to look for man's tasks and possibilities above all on the restricted level of individual action on a small scale. The reason perhaps was that morality was given its classical expression at a time when the social tasks of broader dimensions now incumbent on mankind had not yet penetrated so clearly into each one's imagination. Where such tasks appeared on the horizon, it merely led to a sort of special code of law for superiors and persons in authority. The notion of salvation, fellowship and redemption outside the Church must now be re-considered in new dimensions. The Pastoral Constitution on the Church in the Modern World has already summed up some of these tasks: concern for culture, for social and economic life, for politics, for peace and for the building up of the fellowship of nations. Those who devote themselves with all their strength to such tasks — even outside the Church — are working to bring about a new fellowship. With this, openness for "the other" and the actual acceptance of him are taken out of the rather individualistic sphere of the other who lives close by me. The development of the communications media means that I am also brought into contact with others who perhaps live far away from me. The "other" whose call is now heard is for the European of the present day the Negro of South Africa or of the southern states of the U.S.A., the starving Asian or the economically underprivileged inhabitants of Latin America. Everybody who devotes his life, in no matter what proportion, to the accomplishment of such human tasks is bringing about redemption and salvation. Christians have no reason to deny that this is one way in which Christ's redemption takes shape on earth. It can be objected that redemption is a religious and not a "material" event, that it means the overcoming of sin and not of earthly needs. But the dilemma is incorrect. It is precisely in daily, "material" life that the religious dimension is fulfilled. The religious and the earthly are undoubtedly distinct, but they cannot be separated. Hence moral evil — like moral goodness — contains today a world-wide dimension. If a breach of pledged faith towards another is a moral evil, because it means that one has chosen oneself at the expense of another, then the fatal inertia towards men in need cannot be called anything but evil. And conversely, it must be acknowledged with adult serenity that men who take such tasks upon themselves are truly helping to bring about salvation. This is already taking place in many ways. We may think for instance of the committed delegates or presidents who give years of their lives to the trying assemblies of the United Nations Organization, of those who use their technical abilities to devote themselves to underdeveloped regions, of those who further the good of a national community with a strict sense of political responsibility. If we look at things in this way, it will be clear that there is much more salvation, much more incarnate grace outside the Church than one often suspects.

3. Why the Church?

We put the question once more, more urgently than before. If along with Vatican II one accepts with faith and confidence in

115

God's mercy that there is also salvation outside the Church, then it is no longer *a priori* clear what the purpose of the Church may be. But the question can and must be taken further. If the possibility of salvation outside the Church were to make the Church itself problematical, this would also be true of Christ. After all, the Church is convinced that even before the coming of Christ grace and salvation were already present in the world, even outside the people of the covenant. The same doctor of the Church, Augustine, whose teaching on salvation outside the Church was so subtly nuanced, clearly maintained this opinion. Apropos of Job, who is described in sacred Scripture as a non-Israelite, Augustine says: " I do not doubt that God has ordained that we should conclude from this one example that there were also men among other peoples who lived according tho God's will and were pleasing to him. They belong to the spiritual Jerusalem." [98] Orosius, who knew both Jerome and Augustine personally, expressed the conviction that "God does not restrict his assistance to his body, the Church, which receives special gifts from his grace for the sake of the faith of its members, but gives his assistance to all the nations of this earth, in his patient and eternal mercy." [99] Christians believed and still believe in the possibility of salvation for all men, even for those who lived before Christ's coming. What then is the purpose of Christ's appearing on earth? What is the meaning of the fellowship which confesses him as the redeemer?

Some years ago K. Rahner examined a solution which is still of great interest but which has since come to be seen in a much

[98] Migne, *PL*, XLI, col. 610; also XXXVIII, col. 9; XXXIII, cols. 374–6.
[99] *Ibid.*, XXI, cols. 1188–9.

wider perspective.[100] The kernel of his thought may be given as follows. The meaning of the coming of Christ and the meaning of the Church consist in the fact that in Christ and his Church God's offer of grace comes to us in visible historical form. Each man, the whole human race without exception, is created by God *in order to* share his salvation. This divine call does not remain immanent to God, but has from the start an effect in man himself. Man is intrinsically affected by the call, given as it were a certain quality, which he himself is powerless to change. By way of comparison, one might think, for instance, of how a man's life may be given a certain orientation by his education or by the colour of his skin, before he can determine his own position freely. He need not welcome the orientation. As his freedom develops, he may choose another direction. But he must undoubtedly be influenced in his decisions by the determinations which he underwent earlier on. He may not be fully clear about all the factors which determine his life in the concrete. He will always carry within himself a number of predispositions, of which he his barely conscious or not at all. They are there, nonetheless, and they mark his life. Now, according to K. Rahner, all mankind, in so far as it is called and orientated by God to share in his salvation, may be entitled "people of God". The Church is formed by the special group of the "people of God" which has become explicitly aware of this call and accepts it in freedom. Hence, according to this view, people of God and Church have more or less the same relationship to each other as a historical nation has to the organized State which has been set up on this basis. When this

---

[100] *Theological Investigations*, II (1963), pp. 83–94.

theory was first propounded, there were undoubtedly a number of rather obscure points. Initially it seemed in particular that Rahner held that the call by which mankind was determined as "people of God" was a consequence of the incarnation.[101] It then seemed that according to Rahner this determination, which was caused in man by the incarnation of the Son of God, was in the material or the "nature" of man, precisely in so far as this "nature" is distinct from "spirit". There were a number of objections against such a view. It is difficult to see, after all, why the call of man should have only determined mankind in fact since the incarnation and not from the beginning of creation. In the framework of Rahner's thought as outlined above, the question of the purpose of the incarnation and the Church may therefore be answered by pointing out that God's salvific will is visible in Christ, and that faith in Christ discloses and makes concrete what was present in a hidden way in mankind since the creation.

In recent years in particular, the meaning and function of the Church have been also considered in the light of the biblical category of "substitution".[102] Though the starting-point was not so much theological anthropology as in Rahner, the reasoning led to much the same conclusion, though expressed more concretely. It is presupposed that all magical interpretations of "substitution" are to be excluded. It would be a magical way

---

[101] *Ibid.*, p. 88.

[102] J. Ratzinger, *Die christliche Brüderlichkeit* (1960); id., "Die neuen Heiden und die Kirche", *Hochland* 51 (1958), pp. 1–11; id., "Salus extra ecclesiam nulla est", *IDO–C (Information Document on the Conciliar Church)*, 88 (October 1963), p. 5; id., "Stellvertretung", *Handbuch theologischer Grundbegriffe* II (1963), pp. 566–75; L. Scheffczyk, "Die heilshafte Stellvertretung als missionarischer Impuls", *Geist und Leben* 37 (1964), pp. 109–25; D. Sölle, *op. cit.*

of thinking if one wished another to suffer in one's place, while expecting salvation in one form or another automatically, by virtue of such suffering. The Christian notion of substitution or vicarious suffering is that one knows oneself to be linked in solidarity with the sin-ravaged human race. On this basis, one wishes to take on oneself the suffering inherent in sin, for the sake of the fellowship of which one is a member. The Church is then the fellowship of those who are ready to live in special service for the sake of others. This special readiness to serve is implemented both on the practical and on the more theoretical level. In practice it comes down to the fact that the Church must share in the vicarious act of Christ. "To be a Christian means to give up living for oneself and begin to live for others. In this way it becomes clear that the self-sacrifice of substitution and genuine love are ultimately the one way of the Christian Pasch, the Passover from the old to the new being of man."[103] The theoretical implications have been summed up briefly by D. Sölle. "As regards the anonymous or what Tillich calls the latent Church, the institutional Church has the function of bringing it into the light of consciousness. It has to make the faith intelligible and give an account of it. Taking provisionally the place of God, as it were, it must think out the faith and see that it takes form."[104]

As the common denominator of all these efforts to explain the meaning of the Church, one may point to the factor of the visibility of salvation. Inspired by the figure of Jesus Christ, still active throughout history, Christians know that they are called to make his dedicated service a perpetual and present

---

[103] J. Ratzinger, "Salus extra ecclesiam nulla est", *loc. cit.*
[104] D. Sölle, *op. cit.*

reality. It is for this reason alone that they join together to form a "Church". The whole network of institutions exists only to enable this service and hence this salvation to be more effective. But this readiness to work for the coming of salvation in human forms cannot be restricted to the practical level. Though reflection can sometimes be an alibi for action — Luther could speak of the "harlot reason" — man cannot do without it. Hence the effort to give salvation visible form does not mean only the creation of empirically tangible results but also the disclosure of its meaning and purpose. The simple fact of giving names to realities is of itself an exercise of this revelatory activity of man. The same person may be described as an Irishman, a bricklayer, a husband, a father, a son, an employee, a patient or a customer. With each designation a new aspect of this person is disclosed and hence the various ways in which at any given moment he plays a meaningful part in my existence. The various designations bring to light the full scale of significant realities which go to make up the complex reality of man. Even if one rejects as valueless the reflection which is based on such descriptions, one cannot avoid the work of interpretation. To interpret something as meaningless is already an interpretation. To find it necessary to describe something as meaningless is to have taken up a reflective standpoint.

Hence salvation and fellowship grow, when a group of men join together in a conscious effort to promote human fellowship "in the name of Jesus". The very interpretation which they themselves give to their action generates fellowship. By naming things by their names, we make it possible to attain a fuller *communio* than if they were left anonymous, that is, irrelevant, within our actual existence. Fellowship is not just an anonymous crowd. And hence the text already cited from Peter in the Acts is of great importance for the fellowship of faith in the Church. There is no other name given under heaven by which we must be saved than the name of Jesus Christ. Theology, as reflection on common dedication in faith to Christ, will then be simply the elaboration of all the new meanings which the name has attracted to itself in the course of history. Preaching will serve to present the concrete findings of this work of theology in the fullest freedom. It is not a task which is felt as a painful imposition coming from outside, since it springs from the inner dynamism of the dedication of faith itself. The Church confesses, with Peter and John, "We cannot but speak of what we have seen and heard" (Acts 4:20).

The question of how the Church understands its position in the world where it lives along with many other men, may now be answered step by step. First and foremost, the fellowship of the Church believes that it can bring about the presence of salvation and redemption in the world. This takes place primarily by the effort undertaken in common with all other men to realize earthly values. Hence John XXIII urged the faithful "to take part in public life and to contribute to the well-being of all mankind and of their own country". He mentioned such matters as economic, social, cultural and political institutions and also the duty of attaining "scientific competence, technical ability and professional specialization".[105] A Christian does not cease to be a man. This somewhat banal principle implies that the general human task of realizing earthly values is also the task of the Christian. No matter how the non-Christian comes to be conscious of this duty, Christians at any rate have the

[105] Encyclical *Pacem in Terris*, nos. 146 and 148.

conviction that the transcendent God himself has bestowed this task upon him. In the light of his faith, whereby he sees the world and mankind as the expression of God's constantly creative love, he must be thoroughly penetrated by the truth that no form of real earthly salvation, in its very concrete manifestation, can be a hindrance to the salvific will of God, of which it is on the contrary precisely the manifestation.

In this work of realizing salvation on earth, the Christian is compelled by his faith to profess explicitly the truth which animates his actions and to explain the significance which all this has for him. This is precisely the way in which earthly values are realized in their "mystery-character".[106] Reality, taken as opaque factualness, here receives a new dimension and becomes as it were transparent, because it is given a definite name. Hence Paul interpreted married love as a manifestation of Christ's faithfulness. Our fellow-man is loved as the image of God. By cultivating the earth, Christians believe that they are contributing to the coming of the heavenly Jerusalem where God will be all in all. Such interpretation of earthly life is not a specialty exclusively reserved to Christians. Along with the Christian interpretation of human existence there is also, for instance the Marxist one, or the Buddhist, and all rest ultimately on a belief which inspires the choice.

The confession of the specifically Christian meaning appertains to the whole fellowship of the Church and has a two-fold orientation. First there is the preaching which is directed outwards, as the profession of faith. In this respect, we have become more and more modest. We recognize that "the faith" has too often been proclaimed with the help of inappropriate

[106] See above, p. 19.

means, by which it ceased to be the testimony of faith and became a sort of tyrannous imposition. Further, the march of scientific development has left believers bewildered. The scientific way of thinking has its own method and its own system of verification, which cannot be applied to measure the real value of a decision in faith. If one regards as real only what can be verified as such by an exact scientific system, every act of faith which claims to attain *the* true reality must be rejected as non-human. Other systems of verification must be used in the confrontation of the various philosophies of man and life. If it allowed itself to be afraid of the predominance of science and technology, the Church might try to restrict itself to purely internal activities within the Church and not risk any testimony to the faith in the face of the outside world. Only when Christians are fully convinced of the rightness of a committed outward-looking testimony, which still leaves outsiders fully free, can the second orientation of the preaching be properly considered.

The inward-looking expression is found both in concrete acts and in the word of preaching. The faith of the Church is symbolized in the cultic actions of the celebration of the sacraments. Such actions give outward expression to our dedication to Christ and to each other, and hence strengthen it. Where a profound conviction is never uttered, it finally weakens. And a common conviction which is never celebrated and cannot create for itself an adequate expression also fades and wilts. A truly appropriate liturgy is as important today for the vitality of the dedication of faith as is the preaching of the word. The latter, the verbal expression of faith, is suffering from the general devaluation of language.

The giving of expression to the faith of the fellowship is "organized" in the Church. This is not merely understandable, it is practically inevitable. The primitive community was so deeply impressed by the life and death of Jesus that it wished to prolong this experience on earth by means of preaching. In order to remain in existence as a community inspired by this experience, it could not but become articulate in plea and appeal. The provision of suitable forms of expression was naturally entrusted in a special way to certain individuals, who were to preside over the community as its leaders. They performed their task not by reducing the rest to passivity but by summarizing in kernel the forces which animated all, so that all recognized themselves, their faith, in this statement. This course of events is quite natural. A fellowship acts more truly as such and speaks more truly as such when there are men who can comprise and utter the inspiration of the whole fellowship. Everyone is not equally happy in finding the right word or the right gesture. Hence it is well that there should be a distribution of tasks within the Church, corresponding to the variety of charisms as summed up by Paul.[107] Such a division of labour has the function of serving the task of the Church fellowship. In the light of what has been said above, this task may be defined as "service in the cause of salvation in the world, by means of explicit testimony, in word and deed, to faith in Christ".

The question which we reached at the end of our discussion is supremely urgent. Even within the various Churches more and more doubts are being expressed about the value and purpose of an institutionalized Church. This shows the extent to

[107] 1 Cor 12:4–12 and 28.

which the Churches have ceased to be living fellowships of faith and have hardened into more or less obligatory institutions. When the Church finds itself at a loss as regards its own "mystical" character, it will be helpless. When a successful form of orthodoxy separates the "mystical" and the "real" body of Christ, the "mystical" body is practically bound to become a purely external organization. It becomes no doubt as "visible as the Republic of Venice" (Bellarmine) but becomes at the same time less visible to the eyes of faith. Bellarmine, for purposes of historical polemics, passed over the patristic conceptions which could have been more helpful by their affirmation of the Church as a local eucharistic fellowship.[108] He thus canonized a development which had already been present for centuries in ecclesiastical tradition. It is no simple task to bring such a development to an end. To bring about an improvement in the theological climate is child's play compared with the difficult task of straightening out the actual life of the Church. But this is precisely the task with which we are now faced.

The tide can only turn when the fellowship of the Church, no matter how small, consists of believers who are profoundly penetrated by the "mystical" unity of fellowship and Eucharist. The believing man has given away his heart, deliberately, to the mystery of another who has crossed his path. And in that heart, which is inspired by Christ's own ideal of absolute service, he recognizes values which do not stand apart but are to be found in this world. No arguments can rob him of these values, because the heart has a logic of its own. The encounter with Christ makes the world of the believer transparent. Here

[108] H. de Lubac, *Corpus Mysticum* (2nd ed., 1949), p. 285.

125

within the world he will find himself joined in solidarity to all men, he will carry out the process of secularization to the end, but always under the eyes of him whose name discloses to him the hidden meaning of this world. The Church is the fellowship of those who cannot but give testimony together to this meaning.

There is an inimitable passage in Saint-Exupéry which sketches the pattern of such faith. After a flying accident in the middle of the Sahara, he and his mechanic André Prévot start to look for men in the desert. The heat and thirst become unbearable. When they are near to complete exhaustion, an Arab appears. He fails to see them, and their throats are so dry that they can only make hoarse sounds. A second Arab is also not looking in their direction. But he makes a quarter turn and sees them and walks over to the exhausted men. He gives them water and saves their lives. Saint-Exupéry writes: "You who saved me, bedouin of Libya, you will vanish from my memory for ever. I shall never remember your face. You are Man and you stand before me with the face of all men at once. You did not look at us and still you had already recognized us. You are the beloved brother. And I in turn will recognize you in all men. You stand before me clothed in nobility and goodness, mighty Lord who have power to give drink. All my friends, all my enemies, come to me in you and I have no longer an enemy on earth." [109]

Would Saint-Exupéry have thought it wrong for Christians to decipher in Man the features of him who saved us still earlier from death in the desert?

[109] A. de Saint-Exupéry, *Terre des hommes* (1939), pp. 216–17.

INDEX